101 Best Scenes Ever Written

Other Books by Barnaby Conrad

Nonfiction

La Fiesta Brava

Gates of Fear

Death of Manolete

San Francisco: A Profile in Words and Pictures

Famous Last Words

Tahiti

Encyclopedia of Bullfighting

How to Fight a Bull

Fun While It Lasted

A Revolting Transaction

Time Is All We Have

Hemingway's Spain

The Complete Guide to Writing Fiction

Name Dropping

Snoopy's Guide to the Writing Life (with Monte Schulz)

The World of Herb Caen

Learning to Write Fiction from the Masters

Santa Barbara

Fiction

The Innocent Villa

Matador

Dangerfield

Zorro: A Fox in the City

Endangered (with Niels Mortensen)

Fire Below Zero (with Nico Mastorakis)

Keepers of the Secret (with Nico Mastorakis)

Last Boat to Cadiz

Translations

The Wounds of Hunger (Spota)

The Second Life of Captain Contreras (Luca de Tena)

My Life as a Matador (Autobiography of Carlos Arruza)

101 Best Scenes Ever Written

A Romp Through Literature
for Writers and Readers

Barnaby Conrad

Quill
Driver
Books
Q

Sanger, California

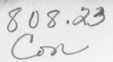
Published by Quill Driver Books/Word Dancer Press, Inc.
1254 Commerce Way
Sanger, California 93657
559-876-2180 • 1-800-497-4909 • FAX 559-876-2180
QuillDriverBooks.com
Info@QuillDriverBooks.com

Quill Driver Books' titles may be purchased in quantity at special discounts for educational, fund-raising, business, or promotional use. Please contact Special Markets, Quill Driver Books/Word Dancer Press, Inc. at the above address or at **1-800-497-4909**.

Quill Driver Books/Word Dancer Press, Inc. Project Cadre:
Doris Hall, Kenneth Lee, Stephen Blake Mettee

ISBN
1-884956-56-4

Printed in the United States of America
QUILL DRIVER BOOKS and COLOPHON are trademarks of
Quill Driver Books/Word Dancer Press, Inc.

To order another copy of this book, please call
1-800-497-4909

Library of Congress Cataloging-in-Publication Data
Conrad, Barnaby, 1922-
101 best scenes ever written : a romp through literature for writers and readers / by Barnaby Conrad.
p. cm.
ISBN 1-884956-56-4
1. Literature, Modern—History and criticism. 2. Motion picture authorship. I. Title. II. Title: One hundred one best scenes ever written. III. Title: One hundred and one best scenes ever written.
PN701.C66 2006
808.2'3—dc22   2006017739

Everything was in confusion in the Oblonsky household. The wife had discovered that the husband was carrying on an affair with their former governess....

The great writers have always practiced this:

Get to a good scene as quickly as possible in your story telling, no matter what with abstract generalization you start.

Tami Hoag does this in the beginning of the best-selling 1999 thriller *Ashes to Ashes*:

Some killers are born. Some killers are made. And sometimes the origin of desire for homicide is lost in the tangle of roots that make an ugly childhood and a dangerous youth, so that no one may ever know if the urge was inbred or induced.

He lifts the body from the back of the Blazer like a roll of old carpet to be discarded. The soles of his boots scuff against the blacktop of the parking area, then fall nearly silent on the dead grass and hard ground. The night is balmy for November in Minneapolis. A swirling wind tosses fallen leaves. The bare branches of the trees rattle together like bags of bones.

He knows he falls into the last category of killers.

Notice, also, how the author gives us "the weather report" only *after* the dramatic action has caught our attention; the days of starting a story or novel with nothing but detailed weather and setting are over. Charles Dickens spends many pages of the opening of *Bleak House* describing nothing but the fog of London! No characters, no conflict—just fog. It wouldn't work today.

> 66 It's not enough to tell the reader that your protagonist is in love – you must show it. 99

Put a character doing something in the midst of your weather and setting.

Sometimes a scene stays in our minds simply because of the unique dialogue and characterization, such as between the odd couple, Lennie and George, in John Steinbeck's *Of Mice and Men*.

The two are bumming around California, avoiding the law because of "the bad thing" the simple-minded Lennie has done to a girl.

Lennie spoke craftily, "Tell me—like you done before."

"Tell you what?"

"About the rabbits."

George snapped, "You ain't gonna put nothing over on me."

Lennie pleaded, "Come on, George. Tell me. Please, George. Like you done before."

"You get a kick outta that, don't you? Awright, I'll tell you, and then we'll eat our supper...."

George's voice became deeper. He repeated his words rhythmically as though he had said them many times before. He tells Lennie the longtime fantasy of their getting a little ranch somewhere.

"O.K. Someday—we're gonna get the jack together and we're gonna have a little house and a couple of acres an' a cow and some pigs and—"

"*An' live off the fatta the lan',*" Lennie shouted. "An' have *rabbits*. Go on, George! Tell about what we're gonna have in the garden and about the rabbits in the cages and about the rain in the winter and the stove, and how thick the cream is on the milk like you can hardly cut it. Tell about that, George."

"Why'n't you do it yourself? You know all of it."

"No....you tell it. It ain't the same if I tell it. Go on....George. How I get to tend the rabbits."

"Well," said George, "we'll have a big vegetable patch and a rabbit hutch and chickens. And when it rains in the winter, we'll just say the hell with goin' to work, and we'll build up a fire in the stove and set around it an' listen to the rain comin' down on the roof—Nuts!" He took out his pocket knife. "I ain't got time for no more." He drove his knife through the top of one of the bean cans, sawed out the top and passed the can to Lennie.

My thanks to Kathy Carnahan, Shelly Lowenkopf, and Barnaby Conrad III, without whom this book wouldn't be.

Contents

1

Of Scenes

If AN ASPIRING WRITER IS TO BECOME A SUCCESSFUL AND PUBLISHED writer of fiction, he or she must truly understand the concept of "show—don't tell." In other words, it isn't enough to *tell* your reader that your protagonist is brave or a coward; one must *show* the reader that the protagonist is either brave or a coward.

It's not enough to *tell* the reader that your protagonist is in love—you must *show* it. The most economical scene I ever saw to show that cupid's arrow had struck was in an old film called *A Letter to Three Wives*; the big lug of a protagonist (Paul Douglas) drives the pretty girl (Linda Darnell) up to her house, and before getting out she gives him a quick kiss on the cheek. He sits there in a daze, mechanically sticks a cigarette in his mouth, takes out the car's lighter, lights his cigarette, shakes the lighter three times, tosses it out the window as if it were a match, and drives off in a trance. We know he's hooked because no one told us—we were *shown*.

By scenes and scenes alone do writers show not tell. In this book are some 101 of the greatest scenes I have come across in my long reading lifetime. Studying them should constitute a valuable shortcut for would-be writers who cannot take the time to read all the books or see the films and plays from which they are extracted.

So okay, exactly what is a scene? What makes a scene *a scene*?

One could say, glibly, that it is an episode where two or more characters engage in dialogue or actions that display character, that change the course of the story in some way, advance the plot, or change the way we feel about this character or that character. But, on the other hand, all through literature, we have scenes with only one character, or a character and a ghost, like Hamlet and his father's ghost, or with one character and a dog—like Jack London's classic "To Build a Fire" (see page 43), or scenes with only one character wrestling with his inner being such as a Tennessee Williams' character in *Cat on a Hot Tin Roof*. And we even have scenes between a mongoose and a cobra, as in Rudyard Kipling's "Rikki-Tikki-Tavi" (see page 174).

Scenes can be thousands of words long, or just five short sentences, like this opening of the 1994 thriller *The Day After Tomorrow* by Allan Folsom:

> Paul Osborn sat alone among the smoky bustle of the after-work crowd, staring into a glass of red wine. He was tired and hurt and confused. For no particular reason he looked up. When he did, his breath left him with a jolt. Across the room sat the man who murdered his father…

Yes, that constitutes a scene! Not an entire scene, but certainly the beginning of one. We have a setting, two characters, and, most of all, a *happening*.

Is this opening, from Ambrose Bierce's classic short story, "An Imperfect Conflagration," a scene?

> Early one morning in 1872 I murdered my father—an act which made a deep impression on me at the time.

No, while it is a grabber, it is not a scene—it is an idea and a statement, not a scene.

In a like manner is Leo Tolstoy's oft-quoted beginning of his novel *Anna Karenina*:

> Happy families are all alike; every unhappy family is unhappy in its own way.

It is not a scene: it is a thought, an observation, a truism; it is a telling, a generality; but Tolstoy, always a story-teller first and foremost, quickly moves into a real scene that we visualize and participate in instead of merely conceptualize: a dramatic exchange between Anna's brother and his wife which starts out:

The funny thing is that just about all we can quote or remember about Steinbeck's perennial classic novel, play, and film is "something about the rabbits."

What reader can forget the chilling scene from Evelyn Waugh's novel *A Handful of Dust*, where Tony Last's wife, who has a son named John and a lover named John, is told the terrible news that "John has been killed in a horse accident!"

Aghast, she asks which John.

"Your son," is the reply.

"Thank God," she says.

Tony moves out and goes to Brazil, where, in another unforgettable scene, he is captured in the jungle by a crazy old English hermit who will force him to read Dickens to him for the rest of his life. (See page 134 for the complete scene.)

What we remember from the books that are important to us are the scenes that play forever on the screen in our minds.

Like Dorothy Gale confronting and accusing the phony wizard of Oz behind the curtain, who replies pathetically: "I'm really a very good man, but I am a very bad wizard I must admit." (See page 192 for the complete scene.)

Or the very erotic carriage ride in *Madame Bovary* where Flaubert makes the reader conjure up a torrid coupling though we "see" none of it. (See page 77 for the complete scene.)

Or Dashiell Hammett's dramatic ending in book and film to *The Maltese Falcon* where the coveted figurine is discovered to be made only of lead—"such stuff that dreams are made on." (See page 226 for the complete scene.)

Or going way back to Homer and his Ulysses' showing up at the end to thwart the horny suitors of the faithful Penelope and send all to Hades.

These scenes, perhaps read in youth, stay with us all our lives; we may not remember the plot of *A Tale of Two Cities*, but how can we forget Dickens's visceral scene of Sydney Carton's last act and "it's a far far better thing that I do than I have ever done."? (See page 212 for the complete scene.)

My cleaning lady, Viola, saw a copy of *Lady Chatterley's Lover* in my studio and asked to borrow it. She returned it a couple of days later with a note; it just might be the truest critique of that famous novel ever:

"Mrs. Chatterley didn't know what she *wanted*, but she sure knew what she *needed*." Then she added: "That one scene!"

Everyone has his or her favorite scene from a book or play or movie. Sometimes they can remember little else about the work except *that one scene*.

For example, I remember almost nothing about Federico Fellini's great 1960 film *La Dolce Vita* except that extraordinary opening, the giant statue of Christ being helicoptered over the roof tops of Rome. Who would ever forget the scene in the 1967 film *The Wrong Box,* where Peter Sellers, in a period costume, is writing a letter with a quill pen and when he finishes he absentmindedly reaches over the desk to a sleeping white kitten, and uses it to blot the ink on the document.

In a similar vein does one remember anything of the 1976 film *Network* except Peter Finch bawling out, "I'm mad as hell and I'm not going to take this anymore!"? (See page 101 for the complete scene.)

And then there are great films and great plays and great novels where one acknowledges their greatness but cannot cite a single memorable scene.

And why are there no great Shakespeare scenes in this book? Simply because if one included all the great scenes from Shakespeare, there would be room for no others. (Okay, so I couldn't resist—I had to include a favorite little comic bit from *Macbeth* (page 136). When I was first required to read it, at the age of fifteen, someone had to explain the, well, the anti-Viagra part.

We all have our favorites and these in this book happen to be mine, and I fully expect to have left out some of yours, for which I ask for forgiveness in advance—but to each to his own.

2

Beginnings

THERE ARE MANY WAYS TO COMMENCE A STORY, BUT PROFESSIONAL writers know they must capture the attention of the reader quickly; they know that starting with someone just sitting around ruminating on his or her past or present life is *not* the way to go. They start with something *happening*.

Remember that a story is something that happens to somebody and the sooner the happening begins, the better.

The beginning of a novel or a short story is so very important that an aspiring writer should take great care with the way it is done. A dull or careless beginning can doom a work. The writer will not be at the editor's elbow when he picks up the manuscript for the first time; the writer won't be able to say "yes, it's a little slow at first but there's a great scene coming up!"

My mentor when I was beginning to write was the Nobel prize winner Sinclair Lewis. He told me that on board a transatlantic steamer once he was pleased to see a fellow passenger settle in a deck chair with his latest novel. He was less pleased when he saw her read two pages, walk to the railing, and drop the book overboard.

"I'd set out to write a book about the biggest bore who ever lived. It was called *The Man Who Knew Cleveland*, and I succeeded in writing the most boring novel with the most boring beginning ever. You just can't get away with it!"

Editors know that professional writers seldom write a dull first page, or even a bad first paragraph, or even an uninteresting first sentence. Let's look at a few well-known ones, starting with Anthony Burgess's outrageous beginning to his novel *Earthly Powers*:

> It was the afternoon of my eighty-first birthday, and I was in bed with my catamite when Ali announced that the archbishop had come to see me.

How could one not read on?
Some others.
The shortest one, from Mark Twain's *Tom Sawyer*:

> "Tom!"

A longer one, from Thackeray's *Vanity Fair*:

> While the present century was in its teens, and on one sunshiny morning in June, there drove up to the great iron gate of Miss Pinkerton's academy of young ladies, on Chiswick Mall, a large family coach, with two fat horses in blazing harness, driven by a fat coachman in a three-cornered hat and wig, at the rate of four miles an hour.

A more exciting one from Virginia Woolf's *Orlando*:

> He—for there could be no doubt of his sex, though the fashion of the time did something to disguise it—was in the act of slicing at the head of a Moor which swung from the rafters.

An enigmatic but strangely inviting one from Melville's *Moby Dick*:

> Call me Ishmael.

And a humorous one from Peter DeVries' *The Vale of Laughter*:

> Call me, Ishmael. Feel absolutely free to do so.

A succinct one from Allan Gurganus' *Oldest Living Confederate Widow Tells All*:

> Died on me finally.

A classic one from Franz Kafka's short story "Metamorphosis":

> As Gregor Samsa awoke one morning from uneasy dreams he found himself transformed in his bed into a gigantic insect.

A provocative one from L. P. Hartley's novel *The Go-Between*:

> The past is a foreign country: they do things differently there.

An intriguing one from James Baldwin's *Giovanni's Room*:

> I stand at the window of this great house in the south of France as night falls, the night which is leading me to the most terrible morning of my life.

A blunt one from Sinclair Lewis:

> Elmer Gantry was drunk.

A shocking one from Florence Aadland's autobiography *The Big Love*:

> There was one thing I want to make clear right off: my baby [age 13] was a virgin the day she met Errol Flynn.

And one of the most quoted great openings is from a once widely read adventure novel, *Scaramouche*, by Rafael Sabatini:

> He was born with a gift of laughter and a sense that the world was mad.

Of course, as great and memorable and quotable an opening paragraph may be, it must be followed by a scene of substance which will evoke the reader's curiosity and intrigue him enough to continue reading.

Elmore Leonard has written many great opening scenes for his novels, but perhaps the most memorable is the classic opening of his *Freaky Deaky*:

> Chris Mankowski's last day on the job, two in the afternoon, two hours to go, he got a call to dispose of a bomb.
>
> What happened, a guy by the name of Booker, a twenty-five-year-old super-dude twice-convicted felon, was in his Jacuzzi when the phone rang. He yelled for his bodyguard Juicy Mouth to take it. "Hey, Juicy?" His bodyguard, his driver and his houseman were around somewhere. "Will somebody get the phone?" The phone kept ringing. The phone must have rung fifteen times before Booker got out of the Jacuzzi, put on his green satin robe that matched the emerald pinned to his left earlobe and picked up the phone. Booker said, "Who's this?" A woman's voice said, "You sitting down?" The phone was on a table next to a green leather wingback chair. Booker loved green. He said, "Baby, is that you?" It sounded like his woman, Moselle. Her voice said, "Are you sitting down? You have to be sitting down for when I tell you something." Booker said, "Baby, you sound different. What's wrong?" He sat down in the green leather chair, frowning, working his butt around to get comfortable. The woman's voice said, "Are you sitting down?" Booker said, "I *am*. I have sat the fuck down. Now you gonna talk to me, what?"
>
> Moselle's voice said, "I'm suppose to tell you that when you get up, honey, what's left of your ass is gonna go clear through the ceiling."

Yes, there are several sticks of dynamite under Booker's chair set to go off when he gets up, and, as it turns out, he has to go to the bathroom very badly and wants to get up—has to get up—desperately. What reader could resist going on?

And besides being hooked, we have learned a great deal about Mr. Booker in a very short time; obviously he is rich, with all those servants, he's a young felon, he's tough and not very nice, and we even know his favorite color. And when he gets blown up we don't give a damn, but we are curious to find out who thought up the clever way to do it—and why. The story is off and running.

80 ❖ CR

JOHN GRISHAM KNOWS THE IMPORTANCE OF STARTING A NOVEL WITH an intriguing mood-setting interest-grabbing scene. The unique first chapter of his 1999 novel, *The Testament*, is unlike any other in modern literature.

Multi-billionaire Troy Phelan, a bitter curmudgeon in a wheelchair, has written down his last thoughts.

> Down to the last day, even the last hour now, I'm an old man, lonely and unloved, sick and hurting and tired of living. I am ready for the hereafter; it has to be better than this.
>
> I own the tall glass building in which I sit, and 97 percent of the company housed in it, below me, and the land around it half a mile in three directions, and the two thousand people who work here and the other twenty thousand who do not, and I own the pipeline under the land that brings gas to the building from my fields in Texas, and I own the utility lines that deliver electricity, and I lease the satellite unseen miles above by which I once barked commands to my empire flung far around the world. My assets exceed eleven billion dollars.

> 66 The beginning of a novel or a short story is so very important that an aspiring writer should take great care with the way it is done. A dull or careless beginning can doom a work. 99

Troy is not a lovable old man, but he is a clever old man with a plan, a plan of revenge against a group of ungrateful "vultures," greedy ex-wives and their slobby children, who wait below in the same building for authorizing of a new will which will make them all rich.

Troy continues with what will be almost his last thoughts:

> Why should I care who gets the money? I've done every-

thing imaginable with it. As I sit here in my wheelchair, alone
and waiting, I cannot think of a single thing I want to buy, or
see, or a single place I want to go, or another adventure I want
to pursue.

I've done it all, and I'm very tired.

I don't care who gets the money. But I do care very much
who does not get it.

Troy has hired three distinguished "shrinks" to prove he is sane so
that his will can never be disputed.

"They expect me to be somewhat loony, but I'm about to
eat them for lunch."

And indeed he does decisively prove himself sane, and the new un-
read will is then approved by the doctors and lawyers.

I grit my teeth and remind myself of how badly I want to die.
I slide the envelope across the table to Stafford, and at the same
instant I rise from my wheelchair. My legs are shaking. My heart is
pounding. Just seconds now. Surely I'll be dead before I land.

"Hey!" someone shouts, Snead I think. But I'm moving
away from them.

The lame man walks, almost runs, past the row of leather
chairs, past one of my portraits, a bad one commissioned by
my wife, past everything, to the sliding doors, which are un-
locked. I know because I rehearsed this just hours ago.

"Stop!" someone yells, and they're moving behind me. No
one has seen me walk in a year. I grab the handle and open the
door. The air is bitterly cold. I step barefoot onto the narrow
terrace which borders my top floor. Without looking below, I
lunge over the railing.

The novel now goes from first person to third person. It is sometime
later and we learn that in the will that Troy made shortly before his fatal
plunge, he disinherits his ex-wives and families and leaves the bulk of
his billions to an illegitimate daughter who is a missionary in the jungles
of Brazil. But how to find her?

Now the story truly begins—and we are truly hooked.

ଏ ❖ ଌ

IS THERE A MORE MELODRAMATIC BEGINNING TO A CLASSIC NOVEL than that in Thomas Hardy's 1886 *The Mayor of Casterbridge*? Michael Henchard, a young farmer, his wife Susan and their young daughter come to a country fair, where he proceeds to get drunk, as is his wont. There is a horse auction going on, and he voices his opinion:

> "For my part I don't see why men who have got wives and don't want 'em, shouldn't get rid of 'em as these gypsy fellows do their old horses," said the man in the tent. "Why shouldn't they put 'em up and sell 'em by auction to men who are in need of such articles? Hey? Why, begad, I'd sell mine this minute if anybody would buy her!"
>
> "There's them that would do that," some of the guests replied, looking at the woman, who was by no means ill-favoured.

Michael goes on for some time about selling his wife.

> "Will any Jack Rag or Tom Straw among ye buy my goods?"
> The woman's manner changed, and her face assumed the grim shape and colour of which mention has been made.
> "Mike, Mike," said she; "this is getting serious. O!—too serious!"
> "Will anybody buy her?" said the man.
> "I wish somebody would," said she firmly. "Her present owner is not at all to her liking!"
> "Nor you to mine," said he. "So we are agreed about that. Gentlemen, you hear? It's an agreement to part. She shall take the girl if she wants to, and go her ways. I'll take my tools, and go my ways. 'Tis simple as Scripture history. Now then, stand up, Susan, and show yourself."
> "Don't, my chile," whispered a buxom staylace dealer in voluminous petticoats, who sat near the woman; "yer good man don't know what he's saying."

The woman, however, did stand up. "Now, who's auction-eer?" cried the hay-trusser.

"I be," promptly answered a short man, with a nose re-sembling a copper knob, a damp voice, and eyes like button-holes. "Who'll make an offer for this lady?"

The woman looked on the ground, as if she maintained her position by a supreme effort of will.

"Five shillings," said some one, at which there was a sigh.

"No insults," said the husband. "Who'll say a guinea?"

The bidding goes on.

"Four guineas!" cried the auctioneer.

"I'll tell ye what—I won't sell her for less than five," said the husband, bringing down his fist so that the basins danced. "I'll sell her for five guineas to any man that will pay me the money, and treat her well; and he shall have her for ever, and never hear aught o' me. But she shan't go for less. Now then—five guineas—and she's yours. Susan, you agree?"

She bowed her head with absolute indifference.

"Five guineas," said the auctioneer, "or she'll be withdrawn. Do anybody give it? The last time. Yes or no?"

All eyes were turned. Standing in the triangular opening which formed the door of the tent was a sailor, who, unob-served by the rest, had arrived there within the last two or three minutes. A dead silence followed his affirmation.

"You say you do?" asked the husband, staring at him.

"I say so," replied the sailor.

"Saying is one thing, and paying is another. Where's the money?"

The sailor hesitated a moment, looked anew at the woman, came in, unfolded five crisp pieces of paper, and threw them down upon the table-cloth. They were Bank-of-England notes for five pounds. Upon the face of this he chinked down the shillings severally—one, two, three, four, five.

Finally Susan speaks up.

"Now," said the woman, breaking the silence, so that her low dry voice sounded quite loud, "before you go further, Michael, listen to me. If you touch that money, I and this girl go with the man. Mind, it is a joke no longer."

And she means it.

Seizing the sailor's arm with her right hand, and mounting the little girl on her left, she went out of the tent sobbing bitterly.

A stolid look of concern filled the husband's face, as if, after all, he had not quite anticipated this ending; and some of the guests laughed.

"Is she gone?" he said.

"Faith, ay; she's gone clane enough," said some rustics near the door.

He rose and walked to the entrance with the careful tread of one conscious of his alcoholic load. Some others followed, and they stood looking into the twilight. The difference between the peacefulness of inferior nature and the willful hostilities of mankind was very apparent at this place. In contrast with the harshness of the act just ended within the tent was the sight of several horses crossing their necks and rubbing each other lovingly as they waited in patience to be harnessed for the homeward journey. Outside the fair, in the valleys and woods, all was quiet.

Michael wakes up sober the next day and sets out to find his wife and the sailor, and thus is set in motion one of Hardy's most convoluted plots.

Notice the nice touch of the loving horses in contrast to the unloving human act we've just witnessed.

so ❖ og

FEW WRITERS HAVE EQUALED ERNEST HEMINGWAY'S ABILITY TO CREATE simple but arresting beginnings in both his short stories and novels.

From a few short stories:

In the fall the war was always there, but we didn't go to it anymore. ("In Another Country")

Go to it? Our curiosity is aroused.

The door of Henry's lunch-room opened and two men came in. They sat down at the counter. ("The Killers")

Why are we reading about two men coming into a lunch-room if they aren't up to something—are they the eponymous killers? We will read on.

That night we lay on the floor in the room and I listened to the silk-worms eating. ("Now I Lay Me")

Silk-worms?!
Notice also the author's continual avoidance of commas before *and* when connecting two sentences.

It was now lunch time and they were all sitting under the double green fly of the dining tent, pretending that nothing had happened. ("The Short Happy Life of Francis Macomber")

What, we want to know immediately, has happened in this exotic setting that is so bad it can't even be discussed?

"The marvelous thing is that it's painless," he said. "That's how you know when it starts." ("The Snows of Kilimanjaro")

It's the brave protagonist talking to his wife as he lies dying in Africa and we soon find that we must stay the course with him.
The beginnings of Hemingway's novels are often deceptively simple but one finds oneself sucked into the story. Take the beginning of his 1926 novel, *The Sun Also Rises*:

Robert Cohn was once the middleweight boxing champion of Princeton. Do not think I am very much impressed by this as a boxing title, but it meant a lot to Cohn. He cared nothing for boxing....

All right, so he doesn't care for boxing, so why does he do it? I'll keep reading.

> He lay flat on the brown, pine-needled floor of the forest, his chin on his folded arms, and high overhead the wind blew in the tops of the pine trees. The mountainside sloped gently where he lay; but below it was steep and he could see the dark of the oiled road and far down the pass he saw a mill beside the stream and the falling water of the dam, white in the summer sunlight. (*For Whom the Bell Tolls*)

We don't know yet why the man is lying in a forest, but something is going on, and we want to find out what it is. Notice how the author immediately gives us a character to focus on and identify with before giving us a description of the setting, time of day, and the season.

To Have and Have Not, Hemingway's 1936 novel about Cuba, is unique in that it is divided into three parts, the parts being told in the first person, the third person, and finally in the omniscient voice. The first part, entitled "One Trip Across," begins like this:

> You know how it is there early in the morning in Havana with the bums still asleep against the walls of the buildings, before even the ice wagons come by with ice for the bars? Well, we came across the square from the dock to the Pearl of San Francisco Café to get coffee and there was only one beggar awake in the square and he was getting out of the fountain. But when we got inside the café and sat down, there were the three of them waiting for us.
>
> We sat down and one of them came over.
>
> "Well," he said.
>
> "I can't do it," I told him. "I'd like to do it as a favor. But I told you last night I couldn't."
>
> "You can name your own price."
>
> "It isn't that. I can't do it. That's all."
>
> The two others had come over and they stood there looking sad. They were nice-looking fellows all right and I would have liked to have done them the favor.
>
> "A thousand apiece," said the one who spoke good English.

"Don't make me feel bad," I told him. "I tell you true I can't do it."

No one understood the role of *conflict* in every story better than Hemingway—and when one character—be it a housewife or a preacher, wants something badly and another character—be it a mother-in-law or a gangster—stands in the way—

You Have Conflict

In the scene in the novel the conflict quickly escalates between the protagonist, Harry Morgan, and the three men.

> "So you won't?"
> "It's just like I told you last night. I can't."
> "But you won't talk?" Pancho said. The one thing that he hadn't understood right had made him nasty. I guess it was disappointment, too. I didn't even answer him.
> "You're not a lengua larga, are you" he asked, still nasty.
> "I don't think so."
> "What's that? A threat?"
> "Listen," I told him. "Don't be so tough so early in the morning. I'm sure you've cut plenty people's throats. I haven't even had my coffee yet."
> "So you're sure I've cut people's throats?"
> "No," I said. "And I don't give a damn. Can't you do business without getting angry?"
> "I am angry now," he said. "I would like to kill you."
> "Oh, hell," I told him. "Don't talk so much."
> "Come on, Pancho," the first one said. Then, to me, "I am very sorry. I wish you would take us."
> "I'm sorry, too. But I can't."
> The three of them started for the door, and I watched them go.

All of a sudden all hell breaks loose:

> As they turned out of the door to the right, I saw a closed

car come across the square toward them. The first thing a pane of glass went and the bullet smashed into the row of bottles on the showcase wall to the right. I heard the gun going and, bop, bop, bop, there were bottles smashing all along the wall.

I jumped behind the bar on the left side and could see looking over the edge. The car was stopped and there were two fellows crouched down by it. One had a Thompson gun and the other had a sawed-off automatic shotgun.

—and we are off and running.

The novel was made into a film in 1944 starring Humphrey Bogart and Lauren Bacall with a screenplay written in part by none other than William Faulkner, he of the Nobel Prize.

৪০ ❖ ৫৪

IN CONTRAST TO HEMINGWAY'S LAID-BACK BEGINNINGS, LET'S LOOK at Jay McInerney's wordy, punchy, and compelling start of his 1984 novel, *Bright Lights, Big City*.

IT'S SIX A.M.
DO YOU KNOW WHERE YOU ARE?

You are not the kind of guy who would be at a place like this at this time of the morning. But here you are, and you cannot say that the terrain is entirely unfamiliar, although the details are fuzzy. You are at a nightclub talking to a girl with a shaved head. The club is either Heartbreak or the Lizard Lounge. All might come clear if you could just slip into the bathroom and do a little more Bolivian Marching Powder. Then again, it might not. A small voice inside you insists that this epidemic lack of clarity is a result of too much of that already. The night has already turned on that imperceptible pivot where two a.m. changes to six a.m. You know this moment has come and gone, but you are not yet willing to concede that you have crossed the line beyond which all is gratuitous damage and the palsy of unraveled nerve endings. Somewhere back there you could have cut your losses, but you rode past that moment on a comet trail of white powder and now you are trying to hang on to the rush. Your brain at this moment is composed of brigades of tiny Bolivian soldiers. They are tired and muddy from their long march through the night. There are holes in their boots and they are hungry. They need to be fed. They need the Bolivian Marching Powder.

A vaguely tribal flavor to this scene—pendulous jewelry, face paint, ceremonial headgear and hair styles. You feel that there is also a certain Latin theme—something more than the piranhas cruising your bloodstream and the fading buzz of marimbas in your brain.

You are leaning back against a post that may or may not be structural with regard to the building, but which feels essential to your own maintenance of an upright position. The bald girl is saying this used to be a good place to come before the assholes discovered it. You don't want to be talking to this bald girl, or even listening to her, which is all you are doing, but just now you do not want to test the powers of speech or locomotion.

How did you get here?

How indeed?

McInerney is skilled in creating surreal situations. The nightmarish scene goes on—and on.

You have traveled in the course of the night from the meticulous to the slime. The girl with the shaved head has a scar tattooed on her scalp. It looks like a long, sutured gash. You tell her it is very realistic. She takes this as a compliment and thanks you. You meant as opposed to romantic.

"I could use one of those right over my heart," you say.

"You want I can give you the name of the guy that did it. You'd be surprised how cheap."

You don't tell her that nothing would surprise you now. Her voice, for instance, which is like the New Jersey State Anthem played through an electric shaver.

The bald girl is emblematic of the problem. The problem is, for some reason you think you are going to meet the kind of girl who is not the kind of girl who would be at a place like this at this time of the morning. When you meet her you are going to tell her that what you really want is a house in the country with a garden.

Does he find her? We must read on. Raymond Carver called the book "a rambunctious, deadly funny novel that goes right for the mark—the human heart."

3

Purely Visual Scenes

THERE ARE A GREAT MANY SCENES THAT WILL REMAIN IN OUR MINDS forever that do not involve words or dialogue of any sort.

The great authors advise fledgling writers:

Aim for the heart!

It's something Charles Chaplin always tried to do whether developing a comic or serious scene.

One of the most poignant moments in all silent films comes at the end of Chaplin's 1931 *City Lights*. The little tramp has fallen desperately in love with the gorgeous blind florist (Virginia Cherrill) who casually gives him a flower every day. When Charlie overhears her saying that she can't afford the operation that could restore her sight, he robs a bank and gives her the money anonymously; she thinks the money comes from an unknown Prince Charming, a secret admirer, who will claim her eventually. Meanwhile, Charlie does time in prison for the robbery. When he gets out he wanders shyly by the flower stand to worship her from afar. But she spots "a funny little man" and impulsively puts a flower in his hand. The moment her hands touch his, she recognizes her "Prince Charming" from her blind days. He tries to pull away, but now she knows to her dismay that the funny little tramp was her benefactor, and her face registers terrible disappointment, yet also gratitude. Charlie tries to smile as he backs away and walks into the sunset, cane swinging. The End.

For me, it *is* the greatest scene in movie history.

As a frivolous aside, I once had the privilege of sitting next to the charming Virginia Cherrill at a dinner party in Santa Barbara. Chaplin was a famed womanizer, especially of young ones, and I asked Virginia if she had been one of Charlie's loves. "Oh Lord, no," she said, "I was much too old to attract him—I was twenty-two!"

Another great visual comes in Orson Welles' monumental 1941 film *Citizen Kane*.

The Hearst-like protagonist, Charles Kane, is crazy about his mistress, Dorothy Comingore, thinks she has a great operatic voice, and lavishes a fortune on singing lessons for her. Through pull, he manages to get the talentless woman into an opera, and in a tell-tale scene we see her on stage, singing an aria in a lavish setting. As she hits a very shaky high note, the camera leaves her to go up and up and focus on two workmen in charge of lighting; they look at each other and solemnly hold their noses and we know that we need never bother ourselves with the poor woman's career ever again.

No need to describe the wordless shower scene in the film *Psycho* where Janet Leigh is stabbed multiple times and the loudest noise is always the screams from the audience.

And who can forget Meg Ryan's fake orgasm scene in the restaurant in *When Harry Met Sally* and the classic line from a woman at a nearby table: "I'll have whatever she's having."

Still another great visual scene in films had its origin in Charles Jackson's novel *The Lost Weekend*. Made into an Oscar-winning film in 1945, directed by Billy Wilder, it starred Ray Milland as an incurable alcoholic whose girlfriend, Helen, despairs of his ever being able to quit. But he finally swears he is on the wagon forever. In a last scene, after searching his apartment painstakingly for booze, Helen finally believes him and seals her love with a kiss. The moment she leaves, he goes to the window and as the movie ends, we see him hauling in a string, at the end of which is his indispensable bottle of whiskey.

(In a review of the film the great critic, James Agee, ended with this paragraph: "I understand that liquor interesh: innerish: intereshtsh are rather worried about thish film. Thash tough.")

Another "Lost"—*Lost Horizon*, a film made in 1937—has one unforgettable, wordless scene. Based on the James Hilton novel, it tells of five people, victims of a plane crash, stumbling into the strange and beautiful Tibetan land of Shangri-La where perpetual health, peace and longevity reign. Ronald Colman falls in love with the beautiful young Asian,

Lo-Tsen, played by the Mexican actress Margó. (Long before Madonna she was the first one-named actress.) The High Lama warns Colman that she must never leave Shangri-La as she is much, much older than she looks. Colman scoffs at the warnings and decides to return to civilization with Lo-Tsen. In a shocking scene, the moment they leave Shangri-La, the girl ages in a few minutes from seventeen to what appears to be one hundred years old and dies.

> 66 And who can forget the fake orgasm scene in the restaurant in *When Harry Met Sally* and the classic line from a woman at a nearby table: 'I'll have whatever she's having.' 99

This cinematic version of *Lost Horizon* makes for a far more dramatic scene than does the novel. Hilton tells his story through the eyes of a narrator, and the end is much more subtle in the book, and certainly less visual.

Oh, yes, he said instantly, he remembered the case of the Englishman who had lost his memory. Was it true he had been brought to the mission hospital by a woman? I asked. Oh, yes, certainly, by a woman, a Chinese woman. Did he remember anything about her? Nothing, he answered, except that she had been ill of the fever herself, and had died almost immediately....I just asked him one final question, and I daresay you can guess what it was. 'About that Chinese woman,' I said. 'Was she young?'

Rutherford flicked his cigar as if the narration had excited him quite as much as he hoped it had me. Continuing, he said: "The little fellow looked at me solemnly for a moment, and then answered in that funny clipped English that the educated Chinese have—'Oh, no, she was most old—most old of anyone I have ever seen.'

Sometimes—not often—the film version of a scene is better than its genesis.

One of the most remembered, purely visual scenes in film history ends the 1930 hard-hitting war film *All Quiet on the Western Front*, based on Erich Maria Remarque's novel. Seen from the point of view of a young German soldier in World War I, the story is a powerful indictment of all wars. Lew Ayers plays the part of the sensitive, butterfly-loving soldier who goes through horrendous experiences during the war but somehow comes through them. Then, on the very last day of the war, he is still in the trenches when he sees a particularly beautiful butterfly just outside the trench. He stands up and reaches for it. We hear the crack of an enemy rifle, and the fingers clench and the hand slides back out of sight. The End. Directed by Lewis Milestone, it won an Oscar for him and the film.

> "Badges? We ain't got no badges! We don't need no badges!
> I don't have to show you any stinking badges!"

Most film buffs will cite Alfonso Bedoya's as the most memorable scene from the 1940 film *The Treasure of the Sierra Madre*, but there was another, with no dialogue, that helped win another actor an Oscar for Best Supporting Actor.

Walter Huston, father of the film's director, John Huston, played one of the three greedy prospectors in Mexico looking for a great gold-laden trove in the mountains. The other two, Humphrey Bogart and Tim Holt, stand open-mouthed in astonishment, convinced that Huston has lost his mind, when on top of a little rise he suddenly goes into a wild maniacal jig. He has found the gold site!

It is a bravura bit of acting that must be seen to be believed, and no one begrudged his winning the Oscar for it.

Even before the credits in Fellini's *Nights of Cabiria* (1957), we have an intriguing visual scene with no dialogue.

We see a charming waifish girl, the actress Giulietta Masina, frolicking hand-in-hand in the sunlight along a river bank with a handsome young man who is obviously her boyfriend. Such a happy bucolic and romantic scene! They stop a moment to hug and kiss, the boyfriend looks around briefly, then yanks the handbag slung from her shoulder, and knocks her into the river. The camera follows her as she floats downstream, struggling to stay alive, coming to the surface periodically, and the credits roll on top of this action. (She is eventually saved, and the story begins.) The film received the Oscar for Best Foreign Film—deservedly.

So here we have several different moods and emotionally distinct visual scenes—closure, brutality, poignancy—but they have something in common besides surprise:

They elicit an emotional and visceral response in a reader or viewer.

4

Action

ELMORE LEONARD'S WELL-KNOWN PRICELESS ADVICE TO BEGINNING writers

"Try to leave out all the parts that readers skip"

is never more in evidence than in his novel *Stick*.

In this scene, Cecil, the fired chauffeur, has come drunkenly to make trouble for Barry, the employer, who is having a garden party. Stick, the low-keyed protagonist, has been hired to replace Cecil as chauffeur and gofer; now he appears on the scene carrying a can of gasoline:

> Stick walked over to the buffet table. He placed a glass on the edge, unscrewed the cap on the gooseneck spout of the gasoline can and raised it carefully to pour.
>
> Cecil said, "The fuck you drinking?"
>
> Stick placed the can on the ground. He picked up the glass, filled to the brim, turned carefully and came over to Cecil with it. Cecil stared at him, weaving a little, pressing back against the cart as Stick raised the glass.
>
> "You doing? I don't drink gasoline, for Christ sake. Is it reg'ler or ethyl?"
>
> Stick paused, almost smiled. Then emptied the glass with an up-and-down toss of his hand, wetting down the front of Cecil's shirt and the fly of his trousers.
>
> There was a sound from the guests, an intake of breath, but no one moved. They stared in silence. They watched

Cecil push against the bar, his elbow sweeping off bottles, watched him raise the fifth of Jack Daniel's over his head, the sour mash flooding down his arm, over the front of his shirt already soaked. He seemed about to club down with the bottle...

Stick raised his left hand, flicked on a lighter and held it inches from Cecil's chest.

"Your bag's packed," Stick said, looking at him over the flame. "You want to leave or you want to argue?"

Readers like to read about people who are good at what they do no matter what that might be. Readers don't like hapless losers as protagonists. How nicely Leonard has characterized Stick as cool, competent, and brave, all in this brief scene. Leonard is famous for his realistic dialogue; notice how he leaves out words—"the fuck you drinking?"— the way we do in real life.

ဆ ❖ ಙ

So MANY WOULD-BE WRITERS WANT TO WRITE INTERNATIONAL thrillers, yet they haven't done their homework and studied the genre. I would recommend that they start with Eric Ambler, then Ken Follett, Trevanian, Nelson DeMille, and, above all, the early novels of Robert Ludlum.

In a Ludlum novel, a tough but sympathetic hero is created, an immense problem is postulated, and the action moves from tense scene to tenser scene, and on to a smashing climax. Here, from his 1980 thriller *The Bourne Identity*, is a typical taut and suspenseful moment:

"Who *sent* you?" asked the Oriental of mixed blood, as he sat down.

"Move away from the edge. I want to talk very quietly."

"Yes, of course." Jiang Yu inched his way directly opposite Bourne. "I must ask. Who sent you?"

"I must ask," said Jason, "do you like American movies? Especially our Westerns?"

"Of course. American films are beautiful, and I admire

the movies of your old West most of all. So poetic in retribution, so righteously violent. Am I saying the correct words?"

"Yes, you are. Because right now you're in one."

"I beg your pardon?"

"I have a very special gun under the table. It's aimed between your legs." Within the space of a second, Jason held back the cloth, pulled up the weapon so the barrel could be seen, and immediately shoved the gun back into place. "It has a silencer that reduces the sound of a forty-five to the pop of a champagne cork, but not the impact. *Liao jie ma?*"

"*Liao jie...*" said the Oriental, rigid, breathing deeply in fear.

The 1988 film was adequate, but failed to capture the crackling immediacy of Ludlum's prose.

Ronald Reagan appeared in some fifty films, yet only

> 66 Readers like to read about people who are good at what they do no matter what that might be. Readers don't like hapless losers as protagonists. 99

one scene from them comes to everyone's mind—a very powerful one taken almost word for word from Henry Bellamann's sensational bestselling novel of 1940, *King's Row*.

The charming but raffish Drake McHugh (Reagan) has lost both legs at the hips in an accident in the railroad yards. He lies in a coma in the home of his girlfriend, Randy Monaghan. He does not yet know the extent of his injuries.

For three days Randy scarcely slept. She felt that she dared not leave Drake. She knew that she had to be with him when he found out what had happened.

Her face was thin and white and harsh with the effort she made for control. She felt that she must not let herself go for an instant. She must not even look in the direction of any release of her own grief. She was fearful that she might never gain control of herself again. She had not been able really to realize that this unspeakable horror had occurred.

It was late afternoon. She had made some coffee. Her head ached.

Tod came softly down the back stairs.

"Randy!"

"Yes—what—"

"He's waking up, I think. did the doctor say give him another injection this afternoon?"

"No."

"Well, I think he's waking up now pretty soon.|

"I'll go to him, Tod. There's some fresh coffee, if you want some."

Randy set her foot on the first step, and paused. It was all she could do to re-enter that room. She stood for several minutes leaning her head against the door frame. It was then that the dreadful sound came from that upper room. Randy knew even in that terrifying instant that she would never forget the sound of Drake's voice. It was a hoarse scream—almost a yell in which there was horror, and pain, and something worse—sheer animal terror.

She tore up the narrow staircase and flung the door open.

"Drake!"

Drake's eyes were rolling and his face worked violently as if the very bone structure had been shattered. Randy saw with a sick horror that his hands were groping frantically under the blankets.

She almost leapt across the room and seized his hands. "Drake! Drake!"

"Randy!"

"Yes, I'm here, Drake. I'm here with you!"

"Randy!"

"Yes, dear. I'm here."

"Randy—where—where's the rest of me?" His voice rose to a sharp wail.

"Hush, Drake. I'm here with you. You'll get well, now."

He held hard to her shoulders. Little by little he quieted.

"Randy!"

"Yes, Drake."

"It was that accident?"

"Yes, Drake. But don't try to talk about it yet. You'll get well now."

His grasp loosened. She looked fearfully at him. He was quieter now. Very slowly he turned his face to the wall. He did not make another sound.

After the film came out in 1942, "Where's the rest of me?" became a much-quoted line, and later became the title of a biography of Ronald Reagan.

℘ ❖ ℞

F. SCOTT FITZGERALD MAINTAINED THAT:

"Action is character."

He also might have added that to a reader a character is an unknown person who reveals himself through his actions. No one knew this better than Graham Greene, and the following thoughts on the writing of action, or "excitement" as he calls it (from his autobiography, *A Sort of Life*,) should prove valuable to any would-be writer.

> Excitement is simple: excitement is a situation, a single event. It mustn't be wrapped up in thoughts, similes, metaphors. A simile is a form of reflection, but excitement is of the moment when there is no time to reflect. Action can only be expressed by a subject, a verb, and an object, perhaps a rhythm—little else. Even an adjective slows the pace or tranquilizes the nerve.

It is worth reading this passage of Greene's several times.

As to the subject of the adjective, remember Mark Twain's admonition:

"When in doubt, strike it out!"

Movement, action, character...
Once action begins in a scene by Graham Greene, it becomes a

model of stripped tension and economy of words. In his masterpiece of a long short story, "The Basement Room" (made into an excellent film in 1948 with Michele Morgan and Ralph Richardson called *The Fallen Idol*), he has only one short scene of violence. The story is seen through the eyes of Philip, a young aristocratic boy. His idol, Baines the butler, is having an affair with a young woman when suddenly his vicious wife returns home in the middle of the night to trap them. Philip doesn't quite understand everything except that he loves Baines and hates Mrs. Baines:

> He got out of bed. Carefully from habit he put on his bedroom slippers and tiptoed to the door: it wasn't quite dark on the landing below because the curtains had been taken down for the cleaners and the light from the street washed in through the tall windows. Mrs. Baines had her hand on the glass door-knob; she was very carefully turning it; he screamed: "Baines, Baines."
>
> Mrs. Baines turned and saw him cowering in his pyjamas by the banisters; he was helpless, more helpless even than Baines, and cruelty grew at the sight of him and drove her up the stairs. The nightmare was on him again and he couldn't move; he hadn't any more courage left; he couldn't even scream.
>
> But the first cry brought Baines out of the best spare bedroom and he moved quicker than Mrs. Baines. She hadn't reached the top of the stairs before he'd caught her round the waist. She drove her black cotton gloves at his face and he bit her hand. He hadn't time to think, he fought her like a stranger, but she fought back with knowledgeable hate. She was going to teach them all and it didn't really matter whom she began with; they had all deceived her; but the old image in the glass was by her side, telling her she must be dignified, she wasn't young enough to yield her dignity; she could beat his face, but she mustn't bite; she could push, but she mustn't kick.
>
> Age and dust and nothing to hope for were her handicaps. She went over the banisters in a flurry of black clothes and fell into the hall; she lay before the front door like a

sack of coals which should have gone down the area into the basement.

Few writers could equal Greene in the writing of sex scenes, perhaps because he never totally abandoned conflict for passion. Take this brief scene from his 1951 novel *The End of the Affair*. The writer Maurice Bendrix and the beautiful Sarah Miles have fallen deeply in love. He goes to her home and finds Henry, his friend and her husband, in bed with a cold. The two lovers cast caution to the wind.

There was never any question in those days of who wanted whom—we were together in desire. Henry had his tray, sitting up against two pillows in his green woolen dressing-gown, and in the room below, on the hardwood floor, with a single cushion for support and the door ajar, we made love. When the moment came, I had to put my hand gently over her mouth to deaden that strange sad angry cry of abandonment, for fear Henry should hear it overhead.

To think I had intended just to pick her brain. I crouched on the floor beside her head and watched and watched, as though I might never see this again—the brown indeterminate-coloured hair like a pool of liquor on the parquet, the sweat on her forehead, the heavy breathing as though she had run a race and now like a young athlete lay in the exhaustion of victory.

And then the stair squeaked. For a moment we neither of us moved. The sandwiches were stacked uneaten on the table, the glasses had not been filled. She said in a whisper, "He went downstairs." She sat in a chair and put a plate in her lap and a glass beside her.

"Suppose he heard," I said, "as he passed."

"He wouldn't have known what it was."

I must have looked incredulous, for she explained with dreary tenderness, "Poor Henry. It's never happened—not in the whole ten years," but all the same we weren't so sure of our safety: we sat there silently listening until the stair squeaked again. My voice sounded to myself cracked and false as I said rather too loudly, "I'm glad you like that scene with the onions," and Henry pushed open the door and looked in. He was carrying a hot-water-bottle in a grey flannel cover. "Hello, Bendrix," he whispered.

"You shouldn't have fetched that yourself," she said.

"Didn't want to disturb you."

"We were talking about the film last night."

"Hope you've got everything you want," he whispered to me. He took a look at the claret Sarah had put out for me. "Should have given him the '29," he breathed in his unidimensional voice and drifted out again, clasping the hot-water-bottle in its flannel cover, and again we were alone.

Did Henry know? We must read on!

I was fortunate to have dinner with the eminent author in 1960. I was living in Tahiti, he was passing through, someone brought him to my house, and we stayed up most of the night talking. He was fascinating on the subject of writing, but to my discredit I made no notes on the occasion the next day and hence haven't a single idea of what was said.

Moral:

Every writer should keep notes!

5

Adventure

Wнo can forget Robinson Crusoe's thinking he was alone on the desert island for so many years and then coming across the footprint in the sand? What a scene. Amazing as Daniel Defoe's story is, considered by many to be the first novel in the English language, the story of the real Crusoe is even more interesting.

Writers throughout the ages have taken real events and based their works of art loosely on them, starting with Homer and the Trojan War. Defoe's inspiration was a not-very-nice young Scotsman named Alexander Selkirk, a drinker and brawler, who after a physical altercation with his father and brother in 1703, went to sea on a rotting Royal Navy ship, *Cinque Ports*, as the navigator, headed for South America. After several months of disease aboard plus dissension with the twenty-one-year-old new captain, Selkirk said the ship was leaking dangerously, and he demanded to be put ashore on a two-and-a-half by seven-and-and-half mile island off the coast of Chile in the Juan Fernandez Archipelago. (It is now called Robinson Crusoe Island.)

When Selkirk got to the island and found that none of the other men intended to desert with him, he changed his mind and tried to rejoin the ship, but the captain refused to take him back. (Just as well, since the decrepit ship sank a short time later off the coast of Peru, and only a few men survived.)

Selkirk had some provisions, and he was sure he would be picked up by another ship in a few days. He was wrong by four years and four months.

His only companions during that time were some feral goats. Food was no problem—he lived on lobsters and the wild goats. He was finally picked up by a ship of the British Navy and eventually returned to England where he became quite a famous figure. But he was unhappy on land and in civilization, and he went to sea again, aged forty-four, and died "of fever" aboard the *HMS Weymouth* in 1721.

Meanwhile, Defoe had read all he could about Selkirk's experience and published what became a literary sensation, *The Life and Strange Surprizing Adventures of Robinson Crusoe*. Defoe takes great liberties with the facts of Selkirk's adventure and even has Crusoe and Friday going back to England, Robinson marrying, having three children, going to Brazil, China, and Siberia, and finally ending up in England.

Here is the famous footprint scene which occurs some twenty-four years after Robinson's arrival on the island.

It happened one day about noon, going towards my boat, I was exceedingly surprised with the print of a man's naked foot on the shore, which was very plain to be seen in the sand. I stood like one thunderstruck, or as if I had seen an apparition. I listened, I looked round me; I could hear nothing, nor see anything. I went up to a rising ground to look farther. I went up the shore and down the shore; but it was all one, I could see no other impression but that one. I went to it again to see if there were any more, and to observe if it might not be my fancy; but there was no room for that, for there was exactly the very print of a foot, toes, heel, and every part of a foot;—how it came thither I knew not, nor could in the least imagine. But after innumerable fluttering thoughts, like a man perfectly confused and out of myself, I came home to my fortification, not feeling, as we say, the ground I went on, but terrified to the last degree, looking behind me at every two or three steps, mistaking every bush and tree, and fancying every stump at a distance to be a man. Nor is it possible to describe how many various shapes affrighted imagination represented things to me in; how many wild ideas were found every moment in my fancy, and what strange unaccountable whimsies came into my thoughts by the way.

When I came to my castle, for so I think I called it ever after this, I fled into it like one pursued. Whether I went over by the ladder as first contrived, or went in at the hole in the rock which I called a door, I cannot remember; no, nor could I remember the next morning; for never frighted hare fled to cover, or fox to earth, with more terror of mind than I to this retreat.

I slept none that night.

And subsequently Crusoe encounters Friday who becomes his servant but also his friend and the saviour of his sanity, even after their rescue.

He was a comely, handsome fellow, perfectly well made, with straight strong limbs, not too large, tall and well shaped, and as I reckon, about twenty-six years of age. He had a very good countenance, not a fierce and surly aspect; but seemed to have something very manly in his face; and yet he had all the sweetness and softness of an European in his countenance too, especially when he smiled.

Islands have long figured prominently in literature, films and plays— Shakespeare's *The Tempest* for example, Wyss's *The Swiss Family Robinson*, James Barrie's *The Admirable Crichton*, Lina Wertmuller's *Swept Away*, John Fowles' novel *The Magus*, and the Tom Hanks' film *Castaway*.

ꙮ ❖ ꙮ

YOUNG WRITERS OFTEN ASK ME: "HOW DO YOU APPROACH A SCENE?"

At the risk of the charge of vainglory in the company of all the masters in this book, I will take a small, but important, scene from my most recent novel, *Last Boat to Cadiz*, which had its beginning in real life in Spain many years ago.

Why do I pick this scene of all the others that I have written in my books?

Because it doesn't *look*—or seem—important. It is not a *whamdoozler*. But it does what I wanted it to do in the early stages of my story. Let me present it to you and then explain why a calm little scene in what is supposed to be a fast-moving thriller can be so vital.

It's early in the novel; the time is near the end of World War II in Europe. Wilson Tripp, the young protagonist, is the American Vice Consul in Sevilla. Here an American expatriate has come to the consulate and asked to speak to Wilson's boss, Consul Tottle. He and Wilson go to see what the man wants.

> At the counter for the public was a thin black man dressed in a neat, worn, camel's-hair overcoat and an ancient homburg. He rested a silver-headed cane on his shoulder and he wore shoes of cracked patent leather with bows.
>
> The Consul approached him. "What can I do for you, George?"
>
> "Moses, sir," the man corrected gently but firmly. His speech was very Southern and well enunciated. "I am very desirous of returning to the States, sir."
>
> "And you don't have money for a ticket, right?"
>
> "That is correct, sir." He took off his hat and ran his hand over his white hair. "I do not have the fare."
>
> "How long have you been in Spain, sport?"
>
> "Let me see now." The man rolled his eyes ceilingward as he calculated. "Yessir, more than fifteen years, must be all of that. Stranded here back in twenty-nine when the troupe I headed ran out of money."
>
> "Troupe?" Wilson said.
>
> "Dance," the old man said with pride. "The Blacks an' Blues we was called. Before Spain, we were in Paris, the opening act for the Ebony Venus, Josie Baker—"
>
> "A dancer?"
>
> "Yessir, tap and eccentric." He held out the heavy silver head of his cane proudly. "See that there? Alfonso the Thirteenth! He give it to me personally after I performed for him once. That there's the Royal Seal."
>
> A strange look came over the Consul's face. "Can you do this, Moses?"
>
> To Wilson's astonishment, the Consul suddenly put his arms out from his side and did an intricate tap step with surprising agility. He ended with a "hah!", one knee bent and his right arm extended, seeking applause from an audience.
>
> "Hasty Pudding, Harvard," he panted, flushed with pride. "Can you do that?"

"No, sir," said Byrd solemnly. "I don't believe I could do that there one."

"I'll teach it to you one of these days," said Tottle, straightening his tie.

"In the words of the great Fats Waller, sir, one never knows, do one."

"Can you still dance, Moses?"

"A little, sir."

"We might hire you for one of our parties. Let's see you in action."

The black man shook his head. "Been a long time, sir. Gettin' old..."

"Come on, just a step or two."

"Here in this office—and without music?"

"Come on, George," the Consul prodded. "Maybe here's a way to make a little money for your fare to the States. People at the party might hire you, too."

The man hesitated. Then he took off his coat and carefully draped it on the counter. He squared his shoulders. He took his cane and planted it elegantly, almost delicately, on the floor with his left hand. Raising his right he began to snap his fingers with a crack. A soft melodic hum came from his lips and his eyes went closed as a little smile came to one corner of his mouth. He stood more erect and seemed to grow younger before their eyes.

"Doo dah, doo dah," Byrd murmured. "Yeah!" He looked down at the cane as though it were some kind of a magic wand. Slowly, he began to move around it, his feet sliding in an intricate pattern, the soles of his patent leather shoes never leaving the floor, his right hand moving rhythmically as though throwing dice and cracking out the beat. He slithered his way completely around the cane. Then he suddenly yanked up the stick, twirled it like a cheerleader's baton, and his feet burst into a machine gun volley. He tapped up to the counter, back five feet from the counter, then circled still tapping in an ever-increasing staccato. As the rat-a-tat-tat crescendoed, he leapt into the air, came down in the splits, oozed himself up to his feet and made an elegant bow, his brown face glowing and glistening with sweat.

The office personnel clapped in delighted surprise and the Consul said: "Not bad, not bad at all, Mr. Byrd, really great. Tell you what, Moses, you teach me that, and I'll show you some great magic tricks."

"Sounds good to me," Moses panted.

Tottle turned back and cleared his throat. "Now back to business. So, suddenly after twenty years, Mr. Byrd, you want to go back to your beloved America. Why the rush?"

"Well, sir, war's almost over, and my wife—she was Spanish—" he swallowed twice. "She died last week." He cleared his throat. "Spent my last *peseta* on her funeral. I'm not getting any younger, sir, and when my time comes I want to be home. I still got people in Virginia, and I want to die and be buried in them beautiful hills."

"Mr. Byrd, I appreciate that sentiment, and I admire you people, always have. But you must understand that we're not a charity institution. We just don't have the funds for such things."

Wilson thought of the seven-hundred-dollar cocktail reception the Consulate had given a week ago for the Baroness of La Huerta, whose sole distinction was that she'd once been named in *Vogue* magazine one of the world's best-dressed women and was a friend of the Consul's wife.

The black man frowned. "But, sir, if I was to die here in Spain, you would then ship my body home, would you not? How come you can't ship that same old body home when it's still alive?"

"I'm sorry, sport," Tottle said, putting his hand on the black man's shoulder. "I'm afraid we can't do anything for you."

The old man was breathing hard now, and his voice was husky. With a long finger he pointed out the window at the river.

"Sir, if I could just get down to the big port, I know I could get a job on a ship bussing dishes, got friends in Cadiz, and I—"

"What's the real reason?"

"Sir?"

"Spaniards giving you a bad time? Because you're American? And colored? And we won the war?"

The man hesitated and then nodded. "Well, there's that. There is a bad element, Sir, who are bedeviling me and certain other Americans. I got to get out for my life."

"I am truly sorry, Mr. Byrd. Afraid I can't help you."

The Consul started to turn away.

"Mr. Tottle," Wilson said, "don't we have an emergency fund?"

"Yes, we do," said the Consul pointedly. "It's for emergencies."

The Consul walked away, calling back over his shoulder, "Don't forget General Franco this evening."

Wilson turned. "Mr. Byrd, I'm sorry. But give me your address."

The man wrote on a piece of paper and handed it to Wilson. As he put it in his pocket, he noticed that the address was very near Mia's. "I'll do my best," he said.

Moses Byrd gave a sad smile as he put on his overcoat. "I do believe you will, sir, and I thank you."

He shuffled out of the door, and Wilson walked back to his desk, glancing at his watch.

I witnessed this actual scene almost exactly as written, and while it made quite an impression upon me I had to wait some fifty years before I found a place where it would pay off.

No scene should be stuck in a story or novel simply because it's "a nice scene." It must be an integral part of the story, advance the story, "plant" an important detail that will surface later in the narration, or develop character and inter-character relations. The above scene did all of those things for my novel.

First of all, I needed to introduce the reader to Moses, who will be an important figure in the dramatic end of the book. Even his cane will come into play at the violent denouement and needed to be "planted" early. The great playwright Anton Chekhov said "If you have a gun in the first act, it must go off before the end of the third act." I wanted him to be a likeable character, and the fact that he has an unresolved problem elicits a reader's sympathy and interest at once. In real life we don't gravitate to people with problems—in fact readers take people with problems—and the bigger the better—to their bosoms!

If the writer can make a reader like or dislike a character, most of the struggle to characterize a person is accomplished.

I wanted to show the Consul as callous and unlikable, and I believe I succeeded by his attitude toward Moses. In a like manner, I wanted the reader to like Wilson, the protagonist, so that he will be pulling for him in the dangerous situation with an escaping Nazi leader he is soon to find himself in, so I show him being sympathetic to Moses' problem. He will ultimately be responsible for Moses being on "the ship of fools," the boat taking several people down the river to Cadiz, all hostages of the evil Nazi.

So there you have a minor character in a small scene that will later have great importance to the plot and the overall outcome of the book. Though the basic scene was a real one that I witnessed, the novel required that I slant it and tinker with it to mesh with the complicated events my imagination had dreamed up for this particular piece of fiction.

I do not recommend a detailed and rigid outline for a novel. Some writers do, but I do believe in having a pretty firm idea of the final outcome of the story, and I keep that in mind when I write each scene that leads to that end, as I did in the foregoing.

℘ ❖ ℘

WHEN ONE REFERS TO A SCENE IN A BOOK OR A FILM OR A PLAY, ONE generally thinks of an episode between more than one person, a couple of people, say, reacting to their interchange of dialogue which advances the plot and reveals each other's characters. But there are many memorable moments in literature where only one character participates in the scene.

Here is a famous and remarkable scene in which we have only a man, a wary dog, and the weather. A beginning writer can learn a great deal by studying this story, especially the no-frills simple style of the prose.

Jack London, who lived from 1876 to 1916, was influenced by Emile Zola's hard-hitting realism (and, in turn, influenced Hemingway). In 1908 London wrote one of the finest action stories ever written, called "To Build a Fire." Curiously, he had written a far inferior version several years before—which only reinforces the old adage:

> 66 No scene should be stuck in a story or novel simply because it's "a nice scene." It must be an integral part of the story, advance the story, "plant" an important detail that will surface later in the narration, or develop character and inter-character relations. 99

"Stories aren't written; they are rewritten!"

The man—he isn't given a name—is making a routine trek in Alaska alone with his dog. The weather turns bad. The man's attempts to build a life-saving fire have all failed, and he finally realizes he may freeze to death. The story is told in one long, vivid scene.

The sight of the dog put a wild idea into his head. He remembered the tale of the man, caught in a blizzard, who killed a steer and crawled inside the carcass, and so was saved. He would kill the dog and bury his hands in the warm body until the numbness went out of them. Then he could build another fire. He spoke to the dog, calling it to him; but in his voice was a strange note of fear that frightened the animal, who had never known the man to speak in such way before. Something was the matter, and its suspicious nature sensed danger—it knew not what danger, but somewhere, somehow, in its brain arose an apprehension of the man. It flattened its ears down at the sound of the man's voice, and its restless, hunching movements and the liftings and shiftings of its forefeet became more pronounced; but it would not come to the man. He got on his hands and knees and crawled toward the dog. This unusual posture again excited suspicion, and the animal sidled mincingly away.

The man sat up in the snow for a moment and struggled

for calmness. Then he pulled on his mittens, by means of his teeth, and got upon his feet. He glanced down at first in order to assure himself that he was really standing up, for the absence of sensation in his feet left him unrelated to the earth. His erect position in itself started to drive the webs of suspicion from the dog's mind; and when he spoke peremptorily, with the sound of whip-lashes in his voice, the dog rendered its customary allegiance and came to him. As it came within reaching distance, the man lost his control. His arms flashed out to the dog, and he experienced genuine surprise when he discovered that his hands could not clutch, that there was neither bend nor feeling in the fingers. He had forgotten for the moment that they were frozen and that they were freezing more and more. All this happened quickly, and before the animal could get away, he encircled its body with his arms. He sat down in the snow, and in this fashion held the dog, while it snarled and whined and struggled.

But it was all he could do, hold its body encircled in his arms and sit there. He realized that he could not kill the dog. There was no way to do it. With his helpless hands he could neither draw nor hold his sheath-knife nor throttle the animal. He released it, and it plunged wildly away, with tail between its legs, and still snarling. It halted forty feet away and surveyed him curiously, with ears sharply pricked forward. The man looked down at his hands in order to locate them, and found them hanging on the ends of his arms. It struck him as curious that one should have to use his eyes in order to find out where his hands were.

He panics and begins to run.

The running made him feel better. He did not shiver. Maybe, if he ran on, his feet would thaw out; and, anyway, if he ran far enough, he would reach camp and the boys. Without doubt he would lose some fingers and toes and some of his face; but the boys would take care of him, and save the rest of him when he got there. And at the same time there was another thought in his mind that said he would never get to the camp and the boys; that it was too many miles away, that the freezing had too great a start on him, and that he would soon be stiff and dead. This thought he kept in the background and refused to consider.

And all the time the dog ran with him, at his heels. When he fell down a second time, it curled its tail over its forefeet and sat in front of him, facing him, curiously eager and intent. The warmth and security of the animal angered him, and he cursed it till it flattened down its ears appeasingly. This time the shivering came more quickly upon the man. He was losing in his battle with the frost. It was creeping into his body from all sides. The thought of it drove him on, but he ran no more than a hundred feet, when he staggered and pitched headlong. It was his last panic.

He is beginning to accept his fate; freezing to death was not so bad.

Then the man drowsed off into what seemed to him the most comfortable and satisfying sleep he had ever known. The dog sat facing him and waiting. The brief day drew to a close in a long, slow twilight. There were no signs of a fire to be made, and, besides, never in the dog's experience had it known a man to sit like that in the snow and make no fire. As the twilight drew on, its eager yearning for the fire mastered it, and with a great lifting and shifting of forefeet, it whined softly, then flattened its ears down in anticipation of being chidden by the man. But the man remained silent. Later, the dog whined loudly. And still later it crept close to the man and caught the scent of death. This made the animal bristle and back away. A little longer it delayed, howling under the stars that leaped and danced and shone brightly in the cold sky. Then it turned and trotted up the trail in the direction of the camp it knew, where were the other food-providers and fire-providers.

If I had one short story in the great vault of short stories to recommend to almost any writer—but certainly to the writer of action, suspense, or adventure—it would be this story by Jack London. (It should be read in its powerful entirety.)

Here you have one long scene which encompasses the much vaunted "Five C's" (Character, Conflict, Compassion, Choice, and Change) that every great story seems to contain. Here we have a *Character*, not necessarily lovable, but in such *Conflict* with Nature that we have *Compassion* for him and the *Choice* he made to continue his journey in spite of the weather. The *Change* at the end of the story is the biggest of all— his death.

Actually, perhaps the greatest Compassion we feel during this tough, unblinking story is for the dog.

It is hard to make generalities about how much or how little action should be included in a story, since all are so different. *Pride and Prejudice* is not *Treasure Island*; *Catcher in the Rye* is not *Harry Potter.*

A movie director, Budd Boetticher, gave me the best advice about action when he told me this anecdote:

The young director says to Jack Warner, the studio boss: "Wait till you see the beginning of my new film—it'll blow you away!"

They go into the projection room and the film begins. A huge Rolls Royce starts down a precipitous, winding road, it screeches around one corner, then another, barely navigates another, then catapults off a cliff. It falls in slow motion to crash and explode on the beach below. The lights come on and the director exclaims: "See? Isn't that the greatest opening scene?!" Warner flicks the ash off his cigar and says laconically: "Who's in the car?"

That is the question we writers should always ask ourselves before initiating any action scene:

Who's in the car?!

සෝ ❖ ශ

TARZAN OF THE APES TRULY TRANSCENDS AND DEFIES CATEGORIZATION. We'll settle for adventure.

It is lucky no one told Edgar Rice Burroughs what every aspiring writer is advised, to write about what he knows. He knew nothing about anything he wrote about.

One example: Tarzan confronts Asian tigers in African jungles. Did no one *tell* him? The story, however, was such a good yarn that no one cared. Appallingly written by a one-time cowboy, policeman, and gold miner when he was thirty-eight, *Tarzan of the Apes* became one of the largest-selling books of all time when it appeared in 1912. Burroughs followed it with *The Return of Tarzan*, *Son of Tarzan*, and twenty-two more Tarzan books, plus a slew of other books and stories (and there have been forty-three Tarzan films since the first in 1918!). And it has recently become a Broadway musical!

In the crudely written series there are many good action scenes, but the line most quoted—"You Jane—me Tarzan"—does not appear in the book. Here is the way Jane and Tarzan meet in the first of the series.

Jane Porter, a proper young lady from Baltimore, Maryland, is in Africa with her professor father and a team of researchers. One day in the jungle, Terkoz, the vicious king of the apes, spots the beautiful Jane and decides to take her for his mate.

> He threw her roughly across his broad shoulders and leaped back into the trees, bearing Jane Porter away toward a fate a thousand times worse than death.

(I warned you that it was badly written!)
Tarzan manages to swing through the trees and catch up with Terkoz and confront him.

> He still grasped Jane Porter in one great arm as Tarzan bounded like a leopard into the arena which nature had provided for this primeval-like battle.
>
> When Terkoz saw that it was Tarzan who pursued him, he jumped to the conclusion that this was Tarzan's woman, since they were of the same kind—white and hairless—and so he rejoiced at this opportunity for double revenge upon his hated enemy.
>
> To Jane Porter the apparition of this godlike man was as wine to sick nerves.
>
> From the description which Clayton and her father and Mr. Philander had given her, she knew that it must be the same wonderful creature who had saved them, and she saw in him only a protector and a friend.
>
> But as Terkoz pushed her roughly aside to meet Tarzan's

charge, and she saw the great proportions of the ape and the mighty muscles and the fierce fangs, her heart quailed. How could any animal vanquish such a mighty antagonist?

Like two charging bulls they came together, and like two wolves sought each other's throat. Against the long canines of the ape was pitted the thin blade of the man's knife.

Jane Porter—her lithe form flattened against the trunk of a great tree, her hands tight pressed against her rising and falling bosom, and her eyes wide with mingled horror, fascination, fear, and admiration—watched the primordial ape battle with the primeval man for possession of a woman—for her.

As the great muscles of the man's back and shoulders knotted beneath the tension of his efforts, and the huge biceps and forearm held at bay those mighty tusks, the veil of centuries of civilization and culture was swept from the blurred vision of the Baltimore girl. When the thin knife drank deep a dozen times of Terkoz's heart's blood, and the great carcass rolled lifeless upon the ground, it was a primeval woman who sprang forward with outstretched arms toward the primeval man who had fought for her and won her.

And Tarzan?

He did what no red-blooded man needs lessons in doing. He took his woman in his arms and smothered her upturned, panting lips with kisses.

For a moment Jane Porter lay there with half-closed eyes. For a moment—the first in her young life—she knew the meaning of love.

Jane must go back to Baltimore and is betrothed to a man she doesn't love. Meanwhile Tarzan becomes semi-civilized, after all, he is Lord Greystoke underneath that leopard skin, and he has added impeccable English to his first language, Basic Ape. He heads for Baltimore and arrives precisely in time to save Jane from a forest fire near her home and the purple prose continues:

From tree to tree swung the giant figure which bore her, and it seemed to Jane Porter that she was living over in a dream the experience that had been hers in that far African jungle.

She stole a sudden glance at the face close to hers, and then she gave a little frightened gasp—it was he!

"My man!" she murmured. "No, it is the delirium which precedes death."

She must have spoken aloud, for the eyes that bent occasionally to hers lighted with a smile.

"Yes, your man, Jane Porter. Your savage, primeval man come out of the jungle to claim his mate—the woman who ran away from him," he added almost fiercely.

Somehow I prefer "Me Tarzan—you Jane."

While largely laughable to modern readers, the Tarzan books can teach a beginning writer a few things. Most of all—*conflict*! There is conflict or tension on every page.

Secondly, a very important *what-not-to-do*: a writer today should not indulge himself by attempting to reproduce ethnic speech by over-the-top variations in spelling, viz: this dialogue between Jane and her black servant, Esmeralda:

> "Esmeralda! Wake up," she cried. "You make me so irritable, sleeping there peacefully when you know perfectly well that the world is filled with sorrow."
>
> "Gaberelle!" screamed Esmeralda, sitting up. "What is it now? A hipponocerous?"
>
> "Nonsense, Esmeralda, there is nothing. Go back to sleep. You are bad enough asleep, but you are infinitely worse awake."
>
> "Yas, honey, but what's de mater wif you, precious? You acks sorter kinder disgranulated dis ebenin'."
>
> "Oh, Esmeralda, I'm just plain ugly to-night," said the girl. "Don't pay any attention to me—that's a dear."
>
> "Yas, honey; now you go right to sleep. Yo' nerves am all on aidge. What wif all dese ripotamuses an' man-eatin' geniuses dat Marse Philander been a tellin' about—Lawd, it ain't no wonder we all get nervous prosecution."
>
> Jane Porter crossed the little room laughing, and, kissing the faithful old black cheek, bade her good night.

Lawdy, lawdy.

છ ❖ ભ

MARK TWAIN WAS A MASTER AT CREATING MEMORABLE SCENES—A scene about a festive jumping frog contest or a scary episode with a murderous Indian in a cave or a life-saving eclipse of the sun in the time of King Arthur or Tom Sawyer white-washing a fence.

Huckleberry Finn is considered one of the bright gems in literature, and to many people it is the genesis of modern American writing: "All modern American literature comes from one book by Mark Twain called *Huckleberry Finn*," wrote Ernest Hemingway.

At the beginning of the novel Huck is living with his drunken brute of a father and, tired of the beatings, he plans to take off down the river in a canoe he has found and hidden. But how to cover his tracks so that he won't be followed and dragged back? Look how this scene lures you into the story:

> While we laid off after breakfast to sleep up, both of us being about wore out. I got to thinking that if I could fix up some way to keep pap and the widow from trying to follow me, it would be a certainer thing than trusting to luck to get far enough off before they missed me; you see, all kinds of things might happen. Well, I didn't see no way for a while, but by and by pap raised up a minute to drink another barrel of water, and he says:
>
> "Another time a man comes a-prowling round here you roust me out, you hear? That man warn't here for no good. I'd a shot him. Next time you roust me out, you hear?"

Huck gets the idea of what to do from what his father said.

> I took the sack of corn meal and took it to where the canoe was hid, and shoved the vines and branches apart and put it in; then I done the same with the side of bacon; then the whisky jug. I took all the coffee and sugar there was, and all the ammunition; I took the wadding; I took the bucket and gourd; took a dipper and a tin cup, and my old saw and two blankets, and the skillet and the coffee-pot. I took fish-lines and matches and other things—everything that was worth

a cent. I cleaned out the place. I wanted an ax, but there wasn't any, only the one out at the woodpile, and I knowed why I was going to leave that.

He gets the gun and completes the scene.

So I took the gun and went up a piece into the woods, and was hunting around for some birds when I see a wild pig; hogs soon went wild in them bottoms after they had got away from the prairie farms. I shot this fellow and took him into camp.

I took the ax and smashed into the door. I beat it and hacked it considerable a-doing it. I fetched the pig in, and took him back nearly to the table and hacked into his throat with the ax, and laid him down on the ground to bleed; I say ground because it *was* ground—hard packed, and no boards. Well, next I took an old sack and put a lot of big rocks in it—all I could drag—and I started it from the pig, and dragged it to the door and through the woods down to the river and dumped it in, and down it sunk, out of sight. You could easy see that something had been dragged over the ground. I did wish Tom Sawyer was there; I knowed he would take an interest in this kind of business and throw in the fancy touches. Nobody could spread himself like Tom Sawyer in such a thing as that.

Well, last I pulled out some of my hair, and blooded the ax good, and stuck it on the back side, and slung the ax in the corner. Then I took up the pig and held him to my breast with my jacket (so he couldn't drip) till I got a good piece below the house and then dumped him into the river. Now I thought of something else. So I went and got the bag of meal and my old saw out of the canoe, and fetched them to the house. I took the bag to where it used to stand, and ripped a hole in the bottom of it with the saw, for there warn't no knives and forks on the place—pap done everything with his clasp-knife about the cooking. Then I carried the sack about a hundred yards across the grass and through the willows east of the house, to a shallow lake that was five miles wide and full of rushes—and ducks too, you might say, in the season. There was a slough or a creek leading out of it on the other side that went miles away, I don't know where, but it didn't go to the river. The meal sifted out and made a little track all the way to the lake. I dropped pap's whetstone there too, so as to look like it had been done by accident. Then I tied up the rip in the meal sack with a string, so it wouldn't leak no more, and took it and my saw to the canoe again.

It was about dark now; so I dropped the canoe down the river under some willows that hung over the bank, and waited for the moon to rise. I made fast to a willow; then I took a bite to eat, and by and by laid down in the canoe to smoke a pipe and lay out a plan. I says to myself, they'll follow the track of that sackful of rocks to the shore and then drag the river for me. And they'll follow that meal track to the lake and go browsing down the creek that leads out of it to find the robbers that killed me and took the things. They won't ever hunt the river for anything but my dead carcass. They'll soon get tired of that, and won't bother no more about me. All right; I can stop anywhere I want to. Jackson's Island is good enough for me; I know that island pretty well, and nobody ever comes there. And then I can paddle over to town nights, and slink around and pick up things I want. Jackson's Island's the place.

I was pretty tired, and the first thing I knowed I was asleep. When I woke up I didn't know where I was for a minute. I set up and looked around, a little scared. Then I remembered. The river looked miles and miles across. The moon was so bright I could 'a' counted the drift logs that went a-slipping along, black and still, hundreds of yards out from shore. Everything was dead quiet, and it looked late, and *smelled* late. You know what I mean—I don't know the words to put it in.

I took a good gap and a stretch, and was just going to unhitch and start when I heard a sound away over the water. Pretty soon I made it out. It was that dull kind of a regular sound that comes from oars working in rowlocks when it's a still night. I peeped out through the willow branches, and there it was—a skiff, away across the water. I couldn't tell how many was in it. It kept a-coming, and when it was abreast of me I see there warn't but one man in it. Thinks I, maybe it's pap, though I warn't expecting him. He dropped below me with the current, and by and by he came a-swinging up shore in the easy water, and he went by so close I could 'a' reached out the gun and touched him. Well, it *was* pap, sure enough—and sober, too, by the way he laid his oars.

I didn't lose no time. The next minute I was a-spinning downstream soft, but quick, in the shade of the bank.

I need not tell you, that is a *good*, a great scene. Notice how the author doesn't just take the lazy way and say that Huck "took some supplies" from the house—he *itemizes* them. We "see" each one.

Readers like details and specifics in their scenes!

We enjoy seeing every clever maneuver that Huck thinks up to complete his phony murder scene. We always enjoy reading about clever people, resourceful people; not about people who are good at nothing, who can't cope—wimps. We become *involved* with Huck

Why?

First, because he is likable and because he has a big problem, one we can identify with: How terrible to be forced to live with a drunken, abusive, perhaps dangerous, parent.

Secondly, he is doing something about his problem, rather than just whining about it passively.

Twain knew how to depict an action scene, and he knew that action delineates character, and he knew how to tell a story. Writers are first and foremost storytellers, and they do it best in scenes like the above.

War

—

ONE OF THE MOST REMARKABLE ENDINGS TO ONE OF THE MOST remarkable American short stories is Ambrose Bierce's much-anthologized "An Occurrence at Owl Creek Bridge." Though at first it appears to be made up of several scenes, in actuality it is only one very brief one.

The first reading of it is an experience in itself. The second reading, after the shock of the ending, is to show the reader how truly beautifully crafted the story is. In other words, this story may not be the greatest short story ever written, but it is hard to imagine how it could have been improved by a single word or sentence.

Peyton Farquhar, a civilian planter, is being hanged by Union troops during the Civil War for trying to burn the Owl Creek railroad bridge and halt their advance into Alabama. When he is dropped from the bridge, we are led to believe that the rope breaks, and he falls into the river. The soldiers' shots miss him, apparently he makes his way to safety, away from them, and loses himself in the forest. He finally manages to stagger to the gate of his little home where his lovely wife holds out her arms in a joyous welcome.

As Peyton reaches out to embrace her, he feels "a stunning blow" to his neck, sees a "blinding white light," hears "a sound like the shock of a cannon—then all is darkness and silence."

To our dismay, we realize that Peyton has not escaped, that it was all a dying hallucination.

The last line:

Peyton Farquhar was dead; his body, with a broken neck,

swung gently from side to side beneath the timbers of the Owl Creek bridge.

ꙮ ❖ ꙮ

FIRST PUBLISHED IN 1865, COUNT LEO TOLSTOY'S MASTERPIECE, *War and Peace*, is considered by many to be the world's greatest novel. It is massive in concept and execution, but Tolstoy still manages to make the reader care about the lives of the many people who occupy his vast canvas. It is difficult to choose one scene from the many great ones in the book, but here is the account of the mortal wounding of the wealthy Russian prince, Andrei Bolkonsky, at the terrible battle of Borodino near Moscow.

At first Prince Andrei, considering it his duty to keep up the spirits of his men and to set them an example, had walked about among the ranks, but he was soon convinced that this served no purpose, that there was nothing they could learn from him. All the powers of his soul, like those of every soldier there, were unconsciously directed to keeping his mind off the horrors of their situation. He walked along the meadow, dragging his feet, rustling the grass, and contemplating the dust that covered his boots; then he took long strides, trying to step on the tracks left by the mowers; then counted his steps, calculating how many times he would have to walk from one border to another to make a verst; then stripped the flowers from the wormwood growing along the edge of the field, rubbed them between his palms and inhaled their pungent, bittersweet aroma. Nothing remained of the previous day's thoughts. He was thinking of nothing at all. He listened with ears that had grown weary of the same sounds, distinguishing the hiss of flying projectiles and cannon reports, and glanced at the tiresomely familiar faces of the men in the first battalion...."Here it comes...this one's for us!" he thought, hearing the approaching whistle of something flying out of that smoke-filled region. "One! Another! Still another! ... A hit..." he stopped and looked along the ranks. "No, it's gone over....But that one hit!" And he resumed his pacing up and down, trying to take long strides to reach the border in sixteen paces.

A hiss and a thud! Five paces from him a cannonball tore up the dry earth and vanished. A chill ran down his spine. Again he glanced at the ranks. Probably many had been blown up; a large crowd had gathered near the second battalion.

"Adjutant!" he shouted. "Order them not to crowd together."

The adjutant, having obeyed the order, approached Prince Andrei. The battalion commander rode up from the other side.

"Look out!" cried a soldier in a terrified voice, and like a bird in a swift flight coming to earth with a whirr of wings, a shell landed almost noiselessly two paces from Prince Andrei.

The horse, not having to question whether it was right or wrong to show fear, was the first to react, snorting, rearing, and almost throwing the major as it sprang to one side. The horse's terror was communicated to the men.

"Lie down!" shouted the adjutant, throwing himself to the ground.

Prince Andrei hesitated. The smoking shell, which had fallen near a clump of wormwood on the border of the plowed field and the meadow, spun like a top between him and the prostrate adjutant.

"Can this be death?" thought Prince Andrei, looking with unwonted yearning at the grass, the wormwood, and then at the wisp of smoke curling up from the rotating black ball. "I can't die, I don't want to die. I love life—love this grass, this earth, this air..."

Even while he was thinking these thoughts, he remembered that people were looking at him.

"It's shameful, sir!" he said to the adjutant. "What kind of—"

He did not finish. There was the sound of an explosion, like the splintering of a window frame being ripped out, and at the same moment, a suffocating smell of powder, and Prince Andrei was hurled to one side, and flinging up his arm fell face downward.

Several officers ran up to him. Blood poured from the right side of his abdomen, making a great stain on the grass.

Beginning writers might feel that Tolstoy is too lofty for them and *War and Peace* too difficult to learn from, but as one can see, there is nothing difficult about the above scene; the reader is *there* in the battle and almost feels the mortal explosion. What *is* daunting about *War and Peace* is its size. The Russian novelist Ivan Turgenev, stunned by its 125 scenes, 559 characters, and more than half a million words, declared:

"It's not a novel; it's an elephant!"

ॐ ❖ ﷼

ONE OF THE MOST POWERFUL OF WILLIAM STYRON'S NOVELS IS *Sophie's Choice*, and certainly one of the most heart-rending scenes in modern fiction occurs in the last third of the 1972 book.

Sophie and her two young children, Jan and Eva, have been arrested and sent to Auschwitz's death camps. Upon arrival, a German officer, drunk, greets the prisoners and decides who is to go to the right, and live, or to the infamous Birkenau, on the left, and die.

Why Sophie, at first glance, thought he might be an aristocrat—Prussian perhaps, or of Prussian origin—was because of his extremely close resemblance to a Junker officer, a friend of her father's whom she had seen once as a girl of sixteen or so on a summer visit to Berlin. Very "Nordic"-looking, attractive in a thin-lipped, austere, unbending way, the young officer had treated her frostily during their brief meeting, almost to the point of contempt and boorishness; nonetheless, she could not help but be taken by his arresting handsomeness, by—surprisingly—something

> 66 One of the most powerful of William Styron's novels is Sophie's Choice, *and certainly one of the most heart-rending scenes in modern fiction occurs in the last third of the 1972 book.* 99

not really effeminate but rather silkily feminine about his face in respose. He looked a bit like a militarized Leslie Howard, whom she had had a mild crush on ever since *The Petrified Forest*. Despite the dislike he had inspired in her, and her satisfaction in not having to see this German officer again, she remembered thinking about him later rather disturbingly: If he had been a woman, he would have been a person I think I might have felt drawn to. But now here was his counterpart, almost his replica, standing in his slightly askew SS uniform on the dusty concrete platform at five in the afternoon, flushed with wine or brandy or schnapps and mouthing his unpatrician words in an indolently patrician, Berlin-accented voice: "I'd like to get you into bed with me."

Sophie ignored what he was saying, but as he spoke she glimpsed one of those insignificant but ineffaceable details—another spectral trace of the doctor—that would always spring out in vivid trompe l'oeil from the confused surface of the day: a sprinkling of boiled-rice grains on the lapel of the SS tunic. There was only four or five of these; shiny with moisture still, they looked like maggots. She gave them her dazed scrutiny and while doing so she realized for the first time that the piece of music being played just then by the welcoming prisoners' band—hopelessly off-key and disorganized, yet flaying her nerves with its erotic sorrow and turgid beat as it had even in the darkened car—was the Argentine tango, "La Cumparsita." Why had she not been able to name it before? Ba-dum-b-dum!

"Du bist eine Polack," said the doctor. "Bist du auch eine Kommunistin?" Sophie placed one arm around Eva's shoulders, the other arm around Jan's waist, saying nothing. The doctor belched, then more sharply elaborated: "Communists?" And then in his fog he turned toward the next prisoners, seeming almost to forget Sophie.

Why hadn't she played dumb? "Nicht sprecht Deutsch." It could have saved the moment. There was such a press of people. Had she not answered in German he might have let the three of them pass through. But there was the cold fact of her terror, and the terror caused her to behave unwisely. She knew now what blind and merciful ignorance had prevented very few Jews who arrived here from knowing, but which her association with Wanda and the others had caused her to know and to dread with fear beyond utterance: a selection. She and the children were undergoing this very moment the ordeal she had heard about— rumored in Warsaw a score of times in whispers—but which had seemed at once so unbearable and unlikely to happen to her that she had thrust it out of her mind. But here she was, and here was the doctor. While over there—just beyond the roofs of the boxcars recently vacated by the death-bound Malkinia Jews—was Birkenau, and the doctor could select for its abyssal doors anyone whom he desired. This thought caused her such terror that instead of keeping her mouth shut she said, "Ich bin polnisch! In Krakow geboren!" Then she blurted helplessly, "I'm not Jewish! Or my children—they're not Jewish either." And added, "They are racially pure. They speak German." Finally she announced, "I'm a Christian. I'm a devout Catholic."

The doctor turned again. His eyebrows arched and he looked at Sophie with inebriate, wet, fugitive eyes, unsmiling. He was now so close to her that she smelled plainly the alcoholic vapor—a rancid fragrance of barley or rye—and she was not strong enough to return his gaze. It was then that she knew she had said something wrong, perhaps fatally wrong. She averted her face for an instant, glancing at an adjoining line of prisoners shambling through the golgotha of their selection, and saw Eva's flute teacher Zaorski at the precise concealed instant of his doom—dispatched to the left and to Birkenau by an almost imperceptible nod of a doctor's head. Now, turning back, she heard Dr. Jemand von Neimand say, "So you're not a communist. You're a believer."

"Ja, mein Hauptmann. I believe in Christ." What folly! She sensed from his manner, his gaze—the new look in his eye of luminous intensity—that everything she was saying, far from helping her, from protecting her, was leading somehow to her swift undoing. She thought: Let me be struck dumb.

The doctor was a little unsteady on his feet. He leaned over for a moment to an enlisted underling with a clipboard and murmured something, meanwhile absorbedly picking his nose. Eva, pressing heavily against Sophie's leg, began to cry. "So you believe in Christ the Redeemer?" the doctor said in a thick-tongued but oddly abstract voice, like that of a lecturer examining the delicately shaded fact of a proposition in logic. Then he said something which for an instant was totally mystifying: "Did He not say, 'Suffer the little children to come unto Me?'" He turned back to her, moving with the twitchy methodicalness of a drunk.

Sophie, with an inanity poised on her tongue and choked with fear, was about to attempt a reply when the doctor said, "You may keep one of your children."

"Bitte?" said Sophie.

"You may keep one of your children," he repeated. "The other one will have to go. Which one will you keep?"

"You mean, I have to choose?"

"You're a Polack, not a Yid. That gives you a privilege— a choice."

Her thought processes dwindled, ceased. Then she felt her legs crumple. "I can't choose! I can't choose!" She began to scream. Oh, how she recalled her own screams! Tormented angels never screeched so loudly above hell's pandemonium. "Ich kann nicht wahlen!" she screamed.

The doctor was aware of unwanted attention. "Shut up!" he ordered. "Hurry now and choose. Choose, goddamnit, or I'll send them both over there. Quick!"

She could not believe any of this. She could not believe that she was now kneeling on the hurtful, abrading concrete, drawing her children toward her so smotheringly tight that she felt that their flesh might be engrafted to hers even through layers of clothes. Her disbelief was total, deranged. It was disbelief reflected in the eyes of the gaunt, waxy-skinned young Rottenfuhrer, the doctor's aide, to whom she inexplicably found herself looking upward in supplication. He appeared stunned, and he returned her gaze with a wide-eyes baffled expression, as if to say: I can't understand this either.

"Don't make me choose," she heard herself plead in a whisper. "I can't choose."

"Send them both over there, then," the doctor said to the aide, "nach links."

"Mama!" She heard Eva's thin but soaring cry at the instant that she thrust the child away from her and rose from the concrete with a clumsy stumbling motion. "Take the baby!" she called out. "Take my little girl!"

At this point the aide—with a careful gentleness that Sophie would try without success to forget—tugged at Eva's hand and led her away into the waiting legion of the damned. She would forever retain a dim impression that the child had continued to look back, beseeching. But because she was now almost completely blinded by salty, thick, copious tears she was spared whatever expression Eva wore, and she was always grateful for that. For in the bleakest honesty of her heart she knew that she would never have been able to tolerate it, driven nearly mad as she was by her last glimpse of that vanishing small form.

"She still had her *mis*—and her flute," Sophie said as she finished talking to me. "All these years I have never been able to bear those words. Or bear to speak them, in any language."

Notice Styron's attention to telling and specific detail—the rice grains "like maggots" on the German's lapel, the music not just music but "La Cumparsita," the German resembling not just any actor but Leslie Howard, familiar to all readers for his many roles, especially as Ashley Wilkes in *Gone with the Wind*.

ℂ ❖ ଔ

RICHARD SCHICKEL, THE *TIME* MAGAZINE CRITIC, WROTE RECENTLY of the 1980 novel, *The Big Red One*, by Sam Fuller (who also directed the subsequent acclaimed film): "There are very few books or films about combat that so persuasively give the reader or the viewer such an intimate sense of what it is like to fight as a common soldier in a vast military enterprise, of the purely accidental ways the question of who shall live and who shall die is determined, the equally accidental ways in which moments of grace are dealt out to soldiers."

It is a remarkable book of war. Perhaps not as gracefully written as Irwin Shaw's *The Young Lions*, or Norman Mailer's *The Naked and the Dead*, or James Jones' *The Thin Red Line*, but when I read it recently (for the first time) I felt at the end that I'd been through the war in Europe and Africa as a battered soldier. Apparently, while a novel, it is based on Fuller's own experiences.

Here is a sample scene that occurs towards the end of the novel. The small group of soldiers that we care very much about have advanced deep into Germany, and one of them has been killed by a sniper.

Griff stopped when he heard the sniper's bolt action. Slowly he inched forward along the stone slab, surprised how unafraid he was. He didn't even stop when he heard the sniper fire. Griff knew he was not the target. He heard the bullet ricochet below.

Griff continued to crawl until he found a wet rock that he climbed over; below him, hiding behind a jutting parapet, was the sniper with the Mauser.

Griff aimed. He couldn't see the sniper's face. He would get this over with quickly. His finger stopped the squeeze as the sniper moved into the light that came from the opening above them.

Griff kept his aim, but his finger stopped the squeeze.

He heard scraping behind him but didn't turn because he knew it was the Sergeant. When the Sergeant reached him, he waited a moment to catch his breath.

"Spot him?" The Sergeant's words were hardly audible. Griff nodded.

The Sergeant was confused. He moved closer, whispering. "What the hell are you waiting for?"

Griff pointed below.

The Sergeant painfully forced himself into position to fire. He aimed, but he held the squeeze because he sensed Griff's horror. The Sergeant turned. Griff's expression begged him not to fire.

The Sergeant worked his way across the stone ledge until he was fifteen feet directly over the sniper. To jump down on that parapet was too dangerous. It was also ridiculous for him to remain there, an easy target if the kid looked up. Griff scurried backward, making enough noise to trigger the sniper to fire three rounds – enough time for the Sergeant to work his way to a seven-inch ledge. The Sergeant lowered himself slowly, then dropped, falling on the kid who was jamming another round into his chamber. The wind knocked out of him, the kid still had the strength and guts to reach for the Sergeant's eyes with clawing fingers. The Sergeant belted the kid across the face with the back of his hand, seized the Mauser, and flung it down into the black pit.

Followed by the rest of the astonished squad, he dragged the kid all the way down the narrow spiral iron stairway.

The little Nazi with the face of an angel was furious. *"Ich bin Soldat des Dritten Reiches! Hitlerjugend! Ich bin ein Hitlerjunge! Ich verlange, als regelrechter Kriegsgefangner behandelt zu warden, von euch Scheissjudengesindel! Heil Hitler!"*

Note how, whether we know German or not, we get the drift!

The Sergeant hurled the sniper to the ground in front of the castle. The ten-year-old kid wore a *Hitlerjugend* armband with swastika. He wore scuffed black shoes and short pants with suspenders over a dirty blue short-sleeved shirt. His hair was dirty blond and his angry blue eyes were filled with murder. When he jumped to his feet, the Sergeant cuffed him down. Again he got to his feet and attacked the Sergeant. Again the Sergeant cuffed him, this time harder, drawing blood from the kid's mouth.

"Imagine a little weasel like that," said Johnson, "killing Switolski."

Vince saw nothing but a miniature Hitler lying on the ground as he spoke. "What do we do with the little son of a bitch?"

"Shoot him," said Zab. "We're supposed to kill any bastard that kills us."

"He's a goddamn kid," said Griff.

"Makes no difference how little the finger is on a trigger," said Johnson. "I say shoot him."

The kid sensed what they were talking about and, to show that he wasn't afraid to die for Hitler, he told them in German that he was a soldier of the *Hitlerjugend* and that he must be treated as a prisoner of war.

"*Heil Hitler!*" he shouted.

"We'll use his carcass as a warning to all Hitler's kids," said the Sergeant, "that we kill 'em if they kill us."

"That makes sense," said Zab.

"All agreed we shoot him?" said the Sergeant.

They nodded. All but Griff, who was dazed by what the Sergeant said. Again the kid sensed what they intended to do. This time he slowly got to his feet, talking fast in German, telling them he wanted to be executed like a German soldier, not shot down as he groveled in the earth. He wanted to be on his two legs and he didn't want any blindfold. He was honored, he told them, to die for Hitler and the Third Reich.

"*Heil Hitler!*" he shouted again.

He gave the salute.

"He's all yours, Zab," said the Sergeant.

"Why *me?*"

"You said shoot him."

"But why *me?*"

"We've got no time for a goddamn firing squad, Zab, shoot the little son of a bitch."

Zab didn't make a move.

"Vinci?" said the Sergeant.

Vinci didn't shoot the kid.

"Johnson?"

Johnson didn't shoot the kid.

"Griff?"

Griff turned away.

"No volunteers?" said the Sergeant.

No one moved.

The Sergeant lifted his rifle and Griff gasped at the same time the kid gasped. But the Sergeant tossed the rifle at Griff, who caught it. Then the Sergeant began to yank the short pants off and the kid began to yell protests, struggling like a wildcat. Enraged, he knew what was going to happen. But he was helpless and the Sergeant now tore off his underpants to expose the kid's bare ass.

The kid cursed him.

The Sergeant propped the kid across his knee and began to spank him. Each crack sounded like a rifle shot. The infuriated kid took the punishment without a whimper and his rage increased as his ass began to turn pink. He frothed at the mouth in anger; he was being treated as a child instead of as a soldier of Hitler's army.

"*Nein!*" the little Nazi yelled. "*Sie dürfen mich nicht wie ein Kind behandeln! Ich bin doch deutscher Soldat!*"

The Sergeant kep whacking the boy's pink ass.

"*Hören Sie sofort auf, Sie Schweinehund! Sie beleidigen den Führer! Sie beleidigen Deutschland! Ich bin ein Hitlerjunge! Ich bin Soldat! Heil Hitler!*"

The Sergeant kept whacking the flesh that turned red and the two little Nazi cheeks began to show welts. Griff looked at the kid's distorted face and thought about what he had read back at the rest camp in Herve. It was a story about kids in Russia playing on a snow slope, using the frozen bodies of German soldiers as sleds.

Suddenly the little Nazi began to whimper. Then he screamed "*Papi! Papi! Papi!*" Now the little Nazi totally reverted, his tears the tears of a child being spanked by his father for having done something naughty.

The boy cried in the rubble that was all that was left of Hitler's thousand-year reich.

Anyone interested in writing a war story should study this book. And while a great deal of information is gleaned about the campaigns in Africa, Sicily, Italy, Normandy, and Germany, it is our emotional attachment to the Sergeant (played by Lee Marvin in the subsequent film) and his little band that we will remember always. (And notice how, like the protagonist of Jack London's story "To Build a Fire," the Sergeant is not given a first or last name.)

As Sinclair Lewis said to me so tellingly, as he dismissed one of my stories with a wave of his hand:

**"People don't read fiction for *information*
—no matter how interesting—
but for *emotion*."**

7

Romance

ASPIRING NOVELISTS CAN LEARN A GREAT DEAL FROM BOTH screenplays and theatrical productions since plays and films, perforce, must unfold their plots in a series of scenes. The writer cannot simply state "then they fall in love" or "then they fall out of love"—we must *see* how they look and act and speak in a scene or a series or scenes.

Though Noël Coward wrote fine, serious short stories (such as "Still Life," later made into a great film, *Brief Encounter*), he is remembered chiefly for his plays and musical comedies. His name is synonymous with scenes of witty dialogue, yet he rarely sacrifices the thrust of conflict or character development simply to make a bon mot or a quick quip. His 1930 play *Private Lives* is called a comedy, but there are many poignant love scenes, such as the following. The situation is that Amanda and Elyot, a divorced couple, are on their honeymoons on the Riviera with their new spouses. Not only are they staying at the same hotel, but, coincidentally, they have adjoining suites.

Remember that:

> **While it is fatally unwise to *end* a story
> with a coincidence, one may happily *start*
> a story with a coincidental happening.**

This is the dialogue that ensues when Noël Coward's protagonists find themselves alone for a few minutes on the moonlit porch:

There is dead silence for a moment.

AMANDA (*not looking at him*): What have you been doing lately? During these last years?

ELYOT (*not looking at her*): Travelling about. I went round the world you know after—

AMANDA (*hurriedly*): Yes, yes, I know. How was it?

ELYOT: The world?

AMANDA: Yes.

ELYOT: Oh, highly
enjoyable.

AMANDA: China must be very interesting.

ELYOT: Very big, China.

AMANDA: And Japan—

ELYOT: Very small.

AMANDA: Did you eat sharks' fins, and take your shoes off, and use chopsticks and everything?

ELYOT: Practically everything. (*He turns to her*)

AMANDA: And India, the burning Ghars, or Ghats, or whatever they are, and the Taj Mahal. How was the Taj Mahal?

ELYOT (*looking at her*): Unbelievable, a sort of dream.

AMANDA (*facing him*): That was the moonlight I expect, you must have seen it in the moonlight.

ELYOT (*never taking his eyes off her face*): Yes, moonlight is cruelly deceptive.

AMANDA: And it didn't look like a biscuit box, did it? I've always felt that it might.

ELYOT (*quietly*): Darling, darling, I love you so.

AMANDA: And I do hope you met a sacred elephant. They're lint white, I believe, and very, very sweet.

ELYOT: I've never loved anyone else for an instant.

AMANDA (*raising her hand feebly in protest*): No, no, you mustn't—Elyot—stop.

ELYOT: You love me, too, don't you? (*He moves to her*) There's no doubt about it anywhere, is there?

AMANDA: No, no doubt anywhere.

ELYOT: You're looking very lovely you know, in this damned moonlight, Amanda. Your skin is clear and cool, and your eyes are shining, and you're growing lovelier and lovelier every second as I look at you. You don't hold any mystery for me, darling, do you mind? There isn't a particle of you that I don't know, remember, and want.

AMANDA (*softly*): I'm glad, my sweet.

ELYOT: More than any desire anywhere, deep down in my deepest heart I want you back again—please—

AMANDA: Don't say any more, you're making me cry so dreadfully.

Elyot pulls her gently into his arms and they stand silently, completely oblivious to everything but the moment, and each other. Then finally they separate.

There you have a lovely old-fashioned love scene! What a nice line is:

"There isn't a particle of you that I don't know, remember, and want."
How could she resist? (She doesn't. They get back together.)

The beginning writer can learn a great deal from this scene—especially what is *meant* and *felt* contrary to the spoken word.

The play is constantly being revived on Broadway, and a successful film was made in 1931 starring Norma Shearer and Robert Montgomery.

🙰 ❖ ◌

IN JAMES M. CAIN'S 1934 BLOCKBUSTER *THE POSTMAN ALWAYS RINGS TWICE*, things are rather different from Noel Coward's style. Let's say, *very* different.

The first line of the book establishes the hard-boiled language of the story:

"They threw me off of the hay truck at noon."

Frank Chambers is a twenty-four-year-old drifter who lands a job at a "roadside sandwich joint, like a million others in California," run by Nick Papadakis and his tough, hormonal young wife, Cora:

> Except for the shape, she really wasn't any raving beauty, but she had a sulky look to her, and her lips stuck out in a way that made me want to mash them in for her.

Within two short chapters they are lovers. In chapter 3 we learn something of Cora's character, background, and the fact that she is up to no good—in fact, is hinting at murder.

> "Look out, Frank. You'll break a spring leaf."
> "To hell with the spring leaf."
> We were crashing into a little eucalyptus grove beside the road. The Greek had sent us down to the market to take back some T-bone steaks he said were lousy, and on the way back it had got dark. I slammed the car in there, and it bucked and bounced, but when I was in among the trees I stopped. Her arms were around me before I even cut the lights. We did plenty. After a while we just sat there. "I can't go on like this, Frank."
> "Me neither."

"I can't stand it. And I've got to get drunk with you, Frank. You know what I mean? Drunk."

"I know."

"And I hate that Greek."

"Why did you marry him? You never did tell me that."

"I haven't told you anything."

"We haven't wasted any time on talk."

"I was working in a hash house. You spend two years in a Los Angeles hash house and you'll take the first guy that's got a gold watch."

"When did you leave Iowa?"

"Three years ago. I won a beauty contest. I won a high school beauty contest, in Des Moines. That's where I lived. The prize was a trip to Hollywood. I got off the Chief with fifteen guys taking my picture, and two weeks later I was in the hash house."

> 66 The writer cannot simply state "then they fall in love" or "then they fall out of love"—we must see how they look and act and speak in a scene or a series or scenes. 99

"Didn't you go back?"

"I wouldn't give them the satisfaction."

"Did you get in movies?"

"They gave me a test. It was all right in the face. But they talk, now. The pictures, I mean. And when I began to talk, up there on the screen, they knew me for what I was, and so did I. A cheap Des Moines trollop, that had as much chance in pictures as a monkey has. Not as much. A monkey, anyway, can make you laugh. All I did was make you sick."

"And then?"

"Then two years of guys pinching your leg and leaving nickel tips and asking how about a little party tonight. I went on some of them parties, Frank."

"And then?"

"You know what I mean about them parties?"

"I know."

"Then he came along. I took him, and so help me, I meant

to stick by him. But I can't stand it any more. God, do I look like a little white bird?"

"To me, you look more like a hell cat."

"You know, don't you. That's one thing about you. I don't have to fool you all the time. And you're clean. You're not greasy. Frank, do you have any idea what that means? You're not greasy."

"I can kind of imagine."

Notice how we're getting back story here—so important to the reader—while still very much in the present.

"I don't think so. No man can know what that means to a woman. To have to be around somebody that's greasy and makes you sick at the stomach when he touches you. I'm not really such a hell cat, Frank. I just can't stand it any more."

"What are you trying to do? Kid me?"

"Oh, all right. I'm a hell cat, then. But I don't think I would be so bad. With somebody that wasn't greasy."

"Cora, how about you and me going away?"

"I've thought about it. I've thought about it a lot."

"We'll ditch this Greek and blow. Just blow."

"Where to?"

"Anywhere. What do we care?"

"Anywhere. Anywhere. You know where that is?"

"All over. Anywhere we choose."

"No it's not. It's the hash house."

"I'm not talking about the hash house. I'm talking about the road. It's fun, Cora. And nobody knows it better than I do. I know every twist and turn it's got. And I know how to work it, too. Isn't that what we want? Just to be a pair of tramps, like we really are?"

Cora then tells Frank more about her husband, a "soft greasy guy with black kinky hair that he puts bay rum on every night."

She sat there a long time, twisting my hand in both of hers. "Frank, do you love me?"

"Yes."

"Do you love me so much that not anything matters?"

"Yes."

"There's one way."

"Did you say you weren't really a hell cat?"

"I said it, and I mean it. I'm not what you think I am, Frank. I want to work and be something, that's all. But you can't do it without love. Do you know that, Frank? Anyway, a woman can't. Well, I've made one mistake. And I've got to be a hell cat, just once, to fix it. But I'm not really a hell cat, Frank."

"They hang you for that."

"Not if you do it right. You're smart, Frank. I never fooled you for a minute. You'll think of a way. Plenty of them have. Don't worry. I'm not the first woman that had to turn hell cat to get out of a mess."

"He never did anything to me. He's all right."

"The hell he's all right. He stinks, I tell you. He's greasy and he stinks. And do you think I'm going to let you wear a smock, with Service Auto Parts printed on the back, Thank-U Call Again, while he has four suits and a dozen silk shirts? Isn't that business half mine? Don't I cook? Don't I cook good? Don't you do your part?"

"You talk like it was all right."

"Who's going to know if it's all right or not, but you and me?"

"You and me."

"That's it, Frank. That's all that matters, isn't it? Not you and me and the road, or anything else but you and me."

"You must be a hell cat, though. You couldn't make me feel like this if you weren't."

"That's what we're going to do. Kiss me, Frank. On the mouth."

I kissed her. Her eyes were shining up at me like two blue stars. It was like being in church.

As Elmore Leonard has said:

"You can do it *all* with dialogue."

Certainly the above scene does it *all*. Boy, there's no talk of the Taj Mahal in the moonlight here!

And a lesser writer might have devoted a sleazy graphic chapter to what Cain does with the simple line: "We did plenty."

Less was more, much more.

Did you notice that in this long excerpt there is not one "he said" or "she said"? They are not necessary—the reader always knows who is talking.

And certainly there is no "he retorted" or "she sneered" or "she whispered" or "he said sarcastically" or "she chortled." The *way* Frank and Cora say the dialogue is inherent in the words they speak. Elmore Leonard never tells the reader how the character speaks a line, except occasionally using a "softly" or "quietly" or "loudly."

If a line of dialogue is quite different from the way one would expect it to be said by this character, it might be enhanced by describing its delivery, viz.: "I love you," he snarled.

In Hollywood, it's called "against the line." Explanation: unexpected delivery of a line of dialogue from the screenplay's character.

(Two films have been made of the novel, the first made in 1946, starring Lana Turner and John Garfield, is infinitely better than the 1981 David Mamet version starring Jack Nicholson and Jessica Lange.)

☙ ❖ ❧

ONE OF THE MOST TALKED ABOUT ENDINGS OF YESTERYEAR OCCURRED in Noël Coward's 1931 play *Cavalcade*.

It comes after a love scene between young Edward Marryot and Edith Harris, his new bride, as they stand in their evening clothes at the rail of an ocean liner, and it was a shocker to the play-goers of the time.

EDITH: It's too big, the Atlantic, isn't it?

EDWARD: Far too big.

EDITH: And too deep.

EDWARD: Much, much too deep.

EDITH: I don't care a bit, do you?

EDWARD: Not a scrap.

EDITH: Wouldn't it be awful if a magician came to us and said: "Unless you count accurately every single fish in the Atlantic you die to-night?"

EDWARD: We should die to-night.

As they exit, Edith picks up her cloak from the rail. It has been covering a life belt labeled "S.S. Titanic."

CURTAIN

The 1933 film made from the play won Oscars for Best Picture and Best Director (Frank Lloyd). And you can imagine with what delight the cameraman zeroed in on the words "S.S. Titanic"!

ℰ ❖ ℬ

THERE ARE SO MANY WONDERFUL SCENES IN EVERYONE'S FAVORITE film, *Casablanca*, that one is hard pressed to pick a favorite. The dialogue is superb and any writer can learn from the screenplay (by Julius and Philip Epstein and Howard Koch).

It all takes places in the louche North African oasis of Casablanca at the beginning of World War II in Rick's Place. Rick, played by Humphrey Bogart, is an American expatriate who still yearns for the love of his life, Ilsa, played by Ingrid Bergman. Rick is a straight arrow, but he is surrounded by corruption, Nazi spies, and vice of all varieties. Here is a famous scene between Rick and the delightfully corrupt police captain, Louis Renault, played wonderfully by Claude Rains.

RENAULT (*loudly*): Everybody is to leave here immediately! This café is closed until further notice. Clear the room at once.

RICK: How can you close me up? On what grounds?

RENAULT: I am shocked, *shocked* to find that gambling is going on in here!

This display of nerves leaves Rick at a loss. The croupier comes out of the gambling room and up to Renault.

CROUPIER (*handing Renault a roll of bills*): Your winnings, sir.

RENAULT: And what in heaven's name brought you to Casablanca?

RICK: My health. I came to Casablanca for the waters.

RENAULT: Waters? What waters? We're in the desert.

RICK: I was misinformed.

Idealistic Rick, it should be noted, ran guns to Ethiopia in 1935 and in 1936 he fought in the Spanish Civil War.

RENAULT: Round up the usual suspects.

Yvonne is a casual girlfriend of Rick's, but he loves only Ilsa. Yvonne has her big moment when the Nazis are singing their patriotic anthem; she leaves the German she's been drinking with to shout out the words to "La Marseillaise."

YVONNE: Where were you last night?

RICK: That's so long ago, I don't remember.

YVONNE (*after a pause*): Will I see you tonight?

RICK: I never make plans that far ahead.

Rick secretly is arranging for papers to get Ilsa and her Freedom-Fighting husband, Victor, on a plane to Lisbon and then the U.S.

RICK: Just the same, you call the airport and let me hear you tell them. And remember this gun's pointed right at your heart.

RENAULT (*as he dials*): That is my least vulnerable spot.

And this tender, brief scene:

RICK: Here's looking at you, kid.

> *This is in a Paris café, a flashback to the day the Germans march in.*

> *Ilsa looks at him tenderly. Rick takes her in his arms, and kisses her hungrily. While they are locked in an embrace the dull boom of cannons is heard. Rick and Ilsa separate.*

ILSA (*frightened, but trying not to show it*): Was that cannon fire, or is it my heart pounding?

These are all great scenes, but probably everyone's favorite is the following one. Ilsa, Rick's great love, left him in Paris. She suddenly appears in Casablanca with her husband. (She had thought her husband dead when she had the affair with Rick in Paris.) It is usually misquoted.

RICK (*drunken nostalgia*): I bet they're asleep in New York. I'll bet they're asleep all over America. (*pounds the table suddenly*) Of all the gin joints in all the towns in all the world, she walks into mine! (*irritably, to Sam*) What's that you're playing?

SAM (*who has been improvising*): Just a little something of my own.

RICK: Well, stop it. You know what I want to hear.

SAM: No, I don't.

RICK: You played it for her and you can play it for me.

SAM: Well, I don't think I can remember it.

RICK: If she can stand it, I can. Play it!

SAM: Yes, boss.

Sam starts to play "As Time Goes By."

At the end, at the airport, Rick is forced to shoot the evil Nazi, Strasser, who is trying to stop Ilsa and Victor's plane from taking off. A police car races up to Renault, who has witnessed the shooting.

GENDARME: Mon Capitaine!

RENAULT: Major Strasser's been shot. (*pauses as he looks at Rick, then to the Gendarme*) Round up the usual suspects.

Renault suggests that perhaps they should both get out of Casablanca for a while.

"Louis," says Rick as they walk off together into the night, "I think this is the beginning of a beautiful friendship."

Perfect!

𝕊𝕆 ❖ ℂℝ

ONE OF THE SEXIEST SCENES IN ALL LITERATURE COULD ALSO BE considered the most chaste, since the reader gets no juicy details, again proving that the most potent sex organ is between the ears. Once again, young writers, less is more!

We are in Paris on a pleasant sunny day with Emma Bovary, the eponymous heroine of Gustave Flaubert's 1856 novel, *Madame Bovary*. Emma and Léon, the younger clerk, get together for their first sexual encounter after longing for each other for some time.

> An urchin was playing in the square:
> "Go get me a cab!"
> The youngster vanished like a shot up the Rue des Quatre-

Vents, and for a few minutes they were left alone, face to face
and a little embarrassed.

"Oh Léon! Really—I don't know whether I should…!"
she said, a little coyly. Then, putting on a serious tone:

"It's very improper, you know."

"What's improper about it?" retorted the clerk. "Everybody does it in Paris!"

It was an irresistible and clinching argument.

But there was no sign of a cab. Léon was terrified that
she'd retreat into the church. Finally the cab appeared.

"Drive past the north door, at least!" the verger called out
from the entrance. "Take a look at the Resurrection, the Last
Judgment, Paradise, King David, and the souls of the damned
in the flames of hell!"

But sight-seeing is not paramount on the couple's agenda.

"Where does Monsieur wish to go?" asked the coachman.

"Anywhere!" said Léon, pushing Emma into the carriage.
And the lumbering contraption rolled away.

It went down the Rue Grand-Pont, crossed the Place des
Arts, the Quai Napoléon and the Pont Neuf, and stopped in
front of the statue of Pierre Corneille.

"Keep going!" called a voice from within.

It started off again, and gathering speed on the down grade
beyond the Carrefour Lafayette it came galloping up to the rail-
way station.

"No! Straight on!" gasped the same voice.

Rattling out through the station gates, the cab soon
turned into the Boulevard, where it proceeded at a gentle
trot between the double row of tall elms. The coachman
wiped his brow, stowed his leather hat between his legs, and
veered the cab off beyond the side lanes to the grass strip
along the river front.

It continued along the river on the cobbled towing path
for a long time in the direction of Oyssel, leaving the islands
behind.

But suddenly it rushed off through Quatre-Mares,

Sotteville, the Grande-Chaussée, the Rue d'Elbeuf, and made its third stop—this time at the Jardin des Plantes.

And so our two fun-seekers continue their amorous endurance contest.

From his seat the coachman now and again cast longing glances at a café. He couldn't imagine what restless craving for movement was making these people persist in refusing to stop. He tried a few times, only to hear immediate angry exclamations from behind. So he lashed anew at his two sweating nags, and paid no attention whatever to bumps in the road; he ran into things right and left, past caring—demoralized, and almost weeping with thirst, fatigue, and despair.

Along the river from amidst the wagons and the barrels, along the streets, the bourgeois on the corners stared wide-eyed at this unheard of spectacle—a carriage with drawn blinds that kept appearing and reappearing, sealed tighter than a tomb and tossing like a ship.

At a certain moment in the early afternoon, when the sun was blazing down most fiercely on the old silver-plated lamps, a bare hand appeared from under the little yellow cloth curtains and threw out some torn scraps of paper. The wind caught them and scattered them, and they alighted at a distance, like white butterflies, on a field of flowering red clover.

Finally, at about six o'clock, the carriage stopped in a side street near the Place Beauvoisine. A woman got out and walked off, her veil down, without a backward glance.

When the novel was published, it made a great scandal and Flaubert was jailed briefly.

A year after *Madame Bovary* was published, cabs for sexual dalliance appeared in Hamburg, Germany.

They were dubbed "bovaries."

℘ ❖ ℃

WHEN I WAS TWENTY-FIVE YEARS OLD, RECENTLY RETURNED TO California from adventuring in Spain and Peru, I met the great novelist

Sinclair Lewis, America's first Nobel Prize winner for literature. When I told him I was trying to finish a novel, he asked to see the first seventy-five pages. The next day he advised me to throw away the first seventy-two pages—"no conflict!" But he saw some merit in subsequent pages and hired me to go to his home in Massachusetts as his secretary. "Before you do any more work on that novel," he said, handing me a book, "every would-be writer must read this book."

Written in 1915, *Of Human Bondage* is generally considered to be W. Somerset Maugham's masterpiece. Though called a novel, this splendid book is largely autobiographical. The hero, Philip Carey, a medical student, has a club foot (Maugham had a hated, life-long, crippling, stammer). Philip encounters, and falls desperately in love with, Mildred Rogers, a pretty but graceless, insensitive, vulgar waitress who uses and only barely tolerates him, in spite of his generosity, devotion, and self-sacrifices for her. Even when she uses what little money he has to run off with other men, he takes in her and her illegitimate baby. His obsessive love for her, which he cannot even explain to himself, never diminishes. They break up, she hits bottom and turns to prostitution, and he still takes her back. "He hated her, he despised her, he loved her with all his heart."

Their dramatic final scene together, when he has finally almost managed to get her out of his system, provided a scene to help Bette Davis become a major film star in the 1934 film. Leslie Howard was Philip in this pivotal scene taken from the novel.

In desperation towards the end of the novel, Mildred tries to wheedle her way back into Philip's affections when he returns to the apartment they share:

> "Can I sit down?" she said.
>
> Before he could answer she settled herself on his knees.
>
> "If you're not going to bed you'd better go and put on a dressing gown."
>
> "Oh, I'm all right as I am." Then putting her arms round his neck, she placed her face against his and said: "Why are you so horrid to me, Phil?"
>
> He tried to get up, but she would not let him.
>
> "I do love you, Philip," she said.
>
> "Don't talk damned rot."

"It isn't, it's true. I can't live without you. I want you."

He released himself from her arms.

"Please get up. You're making a fool of yourself and you're making me feel a perfect idiot."

"I love you, Philip. I want to make up for all the harm I did you. I can't go on like this, it's not in human nature."

He slipped out of the chair and left her in it.

"I'm very sorry, but it's too late."

She gave a heart-rending sob.

"But why? How can you be so cruel?"

"I suppose it's because I loved you too much. I wore the passion out. The thought of anything of that sort horrifies me. I can't look at you now without thinking of Emil and Griffiths. One can't help those things, I suppose it's just nerves."

She seized his hand and covered it with kisses.

"Don't," he cried.

She sank back into the chair.

"I can't go on like this. If you won't love me, I'd rather go away."

"Don't be foolish, you haven't anywhere to go. You can stay here as long as you like, but it must be on the definite understanding that we're friends and nothing more."

Then she dropped suddenly the vehemence of passion and gave a soft, insinuating laugh. She sidled up to Philip and put her arms round him. She made her voice low and wheedling.

"Don't be such an old silly. I believe you're nervous. You don't know how nice I can be."

She put her face against his and rubbed his cheek with hers. To Philip her smile was an abominable leer, and the suggestive glitter of her eyes filled him with horror. He drew back instinctively.

"I won't," he said.

But she would not let him go. She sought his mouth with her lips. He took her hands and tore them roughly apart and pushed her away.

"You disgust me," he said.

"Me?"

She steadied herself with one hand on the chimney-piece.

She looked at him for an instant, and two red spots suddenly appeared on her cheeks. She gave a shrill, angry laugh.

"I disgust *you*."

She paused and drew in her breath sharply. Then she burst into a furious torrent of abuse. She shouted at the top of her voice. She called him every foul name she could think of. She used language so obscene that Philip was astounded; she was always so anxious to be refined, so shocked by coarseness, that it had never occurred to him that she knew the words she used now. She came up to him and thrust her face in his. It was distorted with passion, and in her tumultuous speech the spittle dribbled over her lips.

"I never cared for you, not once, I was making a fool of you always, you bored me, you bored me stiff, and I hated you, I would never have let you touch me only for the money, and it used to make me sick when I had to let you kiss me. We laughed at you, Griffiths and me, we laughed because you was such a mug. A mug! A mug!"

Then she burst again into abominable invective. She accused him of every mean fault; she said he was stingy, she said he was dull, she said he was vain selfish; she cast virulent ridicule on everything upon which he was most sensitive. And at last she turned to go. She kept on, with hysterical violence, shouting at him an opprobrious, filthy epithet. She seized the hand of the door and flung it open. Then she turned round and hurled at him the injury which she knew was the only one that really touched him. She threw into the word all the malice and all the venom of which she was capable. She flung it at him as though it were a blow.

"Cripple!"

The scene in the film follows the one in the novel almost exactly, except that Bette Davis, or the director, John Cromwell, embellished the diatribe with this cockney line:

MILDRED: And, when you kissed me, I woiped moy mouth, (demonstrates, wiping lips with back of hand) woiped moy mouth!

As I was reading the book, entranced, Sinclair Lewis remarked off-handedly to me: "You'll understand and appreciate *Of Human Bondage* better if you keep in mind that Mildred in real life was a man."

Once Maugham, at the end of a fancy dinner party in London, stood up from the table, saying to his hostess as he did:

"Well, my dear, I'd best be off to bed if I'm to keep my youth."

"Why, Willie," she admonished, "you should have brought him!"

⅋ ❖ ⅌

MARTY, BY PADDY CHAYEFSKY, WAS A ROMANCE LIKE NONE AUDIENCES had ever seen before. It came on television's small screen in 1953 and was the talk of the entertainment world the next day—and for days and months afterwards. The author said of it:

"I set out in *Marty* to write a love story, the most ordinary love story in the world. I didn't want my hero to be handsome, and I didn't want the girl to be pretty. I wanted to write a love story the way it would literally have happened to the kind of people I know."

Marty, a kind but physically unattractive butcher, very shy with girls, has met a lonely, nice but physically plain woman at a dance the night before. They get along very well. As he does every Saturday, he meets with his buddies at the same bar, all unmarried, always asking in boredom "so—whatta ya want to do tonight?"

> ANGIE: Listen, Marty, I gotta good place for us to go tonight. The kid here, he says, he was downna bazaar at Our Lady of Angels last night and...
>
> MARTY: I don't feel like going to the bazaar, Angie. I thought I'd take this girl to a movie.
>
> ANGIE: Boy, you really musta made out good last night.
>
> MARTY: We just talked.
>
> ANGIE: Boy, she must be some talker. She musta been about fifty years old.

THE CRITIC: I always figger a guy oughtta marry a girl who's twenny years younger than he is, so that when he's forty, his wife is a real nice-looking doll.

THE TWENTY-YEAR-OLD: That means he'd have to marry the girl when she was one year old.

THE CRITIC: I never thoughta that.

Marty is wrestling with what he truly feels against "public opinion," which he's always listened to.

MARTY: I didn't think she was so bad-looking.

ANGIE: She musta kept you inna shadows all night.

THE CRITIC: Marty, you don't wanna hang around with dogs. It gives you a bad reputation.

ANGIE: Marty, let's go downna bazaar.

MARTY: I told this dog I was gonna call her today.

ANGIE: Brush her.

Marty looks questioningly at Angie.

MARTY: You didn't like her at all?

ANGIE: A nothing. A real nothing.

Marty looks down at the dime he has been nervously turning between his fingers and then, frowning, he slips it into his jacket pocket. He lowers his face and looks down, scowling at his thoughts. Around him, the voices go along.

THE CRITIC: What's playing on Fordham Road? I think there's a good picture in Loew's Paradise.

ANGIE: Let's go down to Forty-Second Street and walk around. We're sure to wind up with something.

Slowly Marty begins to look up again. He looks from face to face as he speaks.

THE CRITIC: I'll never forgive La Guardia for cutting burlesque outta New York City!

THE TWENTY-YEAR-OLD: There's burlesque over in Union City. Let's go to Union City....

ANGIE: Ah, they're always crowded on Sunday night.

Now watch how the dialogue changes. Marty is listening to these losers and realizes he's wasting his time with them, that love makes him different and that he's got to grab it.

THE CRITIC: So wadda you figure on doing tonight, Angie?

ANGIE: I don't know. Wadda you figure on doing?

THE CRITIC: I don't know. *(Turns to The Twenty-Year-Old.)* Wadda you figure on doing?

The Twenty-Year-Old shrugs. Suddenly Marty brings his fist down on the table with a crash. The others turn, startled, toward him. Marty rises in his seat.

MARTY: "What are you doing tonight?" "I don't know, what are you doing?" Burlesque! Loew's Paradise! Miserable and lonely! Miserable and lonely and stupid! What am I, crazy or something?! I got something good! What am I hanging around with you guys for?!

He has said this in tones so loud that it attracts the attention of everyone in the bar. A little embarrassed, Marty turns and moves quickly to the phone booth, pausing out-

side the door to find his dime again. Angie is out of his seat immediately and hurries after him.

ANGIE (*A little shocked at Marty's outburst*): Watsa matter with you?

MARTY (*In a low, intense voice*): You don't like her. My mother don't like her. She's a dog, and I'm a fat, ugly little man. All I know is I had a good time last night. I'm gonna have a good time tonight. If we have enough good times together, I'm going down on my knees and beg that girl to marry me. If we make a party again this New Year's, I gotta date for the party. You don't like her, that's too bad. (*He moves into the booth, sits, turns again to Angie, smiles.*) When you gonna get married, Angie? You're thirty-four years old. All your kid brothers are married. You oughtta be ashamed of yourself.

Still smiling at his private joke, he puts the dime into the slot and then—with a determined finger—he begins to dial.

FADE OUT.
THE END

"I tried writing the dialogue as if it had been wire-tapped," Chayefsky said. "I tried to envision the scenes as if a camera had been focused upon the unsuspecting characters and had caught them in an untouched moment of life."

Good advice for a writer of any type of fiction!

The part of Marty on TV was played to perfection by Rod Steiger, and in the subsequent film by Ernest Borgnine, who won the Oscar for his performance.

৪৩ ❖ ୧୪

ANNIE PROULX'S SENSATIONAL SHORT STORY ABOUT THE LOVE OF two Wyoming cowboys, "Brokeback Mountain," was made into an equally sensational film, screenplay by Larry McMurtry and Diana Ossana, in 2005, with Oscars for the screenplay and the director.

In this scene Jack Twist shows up to visit with his lover, Ennis De Mar, at the dingy apartment De Mar shares with his wife, Alma, and his two daughters. Alma has learned of the nature of the relationship and is waiting for Jack when he comes in after a night out with Ennis.

Interior: Riverton, Wyo.: Del Mar apartment.

Alma sits at the kitchen table, disheveled, nervous, hasn't slept all night, a cup of coffee in front of her.
Ennis comes through the door.

Alma stands…confused yet relieved Ennis came back home, struggles with complex feelings. Keeps big emotion inside. Tries to catch his eye.

Ennis tries to ignore her.

Alma looks out the window…sees Jack outside his pickup, he leans against the driver door.

ENNIS: Me and Jack's heading up to the mountains for a day or two. Do a little fishin'.

ALMA *(cautious)*: You know, your friend could come inside, have a cup of coffee…we ain't poison or nothing'.

ENNIS *(as if this is explanation enough)*: He's from Texas.

ALMA: Texans don't drink coffee?

Ennis opens the hall closet. Takes out a duffel bag.

Starts to pack.

Alma's eyes widen…

ALMA: You sure that foreman won't fire you for taking off?

Ennis takes his rod, reel and creel case out of the closet.

ENNIS: That foreman owes me. I worked through a blizzard last Christmas, remember? Besides, I'll only be a couple of days.

Alma Jr. hears her father's voice, stumbles out of the bedroom, rubs sleep out of her eyes.

ALMA JR.: Bring me a fish, Daddy, a big fish.

ENNIS *(to Alma Jr.)*: Come here.

Gives her a big kiss. Turns to Alma.

Awkward.

Gives her a quick one-arm hug, kisses her on the cheek.

ENNIS: See you Sunday, latest.

Leaves.

Alma goes to the window.

Looks out…sees Ennis throw his stuff in the back of Jack's truck. Gets in the passenger side, Jack gets in the driver's side.

Pale, filled with disquiet, anguish, watches them go. Cries.

The power of the scene comes from the understatement, what *isn't* said. Once again, less is more.

If I were asked by a young writer, "I'm trying to write a great sweeping epic about America, what should I read?," I would immediately reply John Dos Passos's *USA* and *Gone with the Wind*.

Margaret Mitchell's first and only novel, *Gone with the Wind*, burst upon the American scene in 1936, the best seller of all time, and still selling. In its 689 pages are to be found many great scenes: Prissy's "Don't know nuthin' about birthin' babies"; Scarlett's shooting the Yankee soldier invading her home; the siege of Atlanta; Little Bonnie's death; Rhett sweeping Scarlett up to bed; and so forth.

But the scene everyone remembers and quotes is the line near the end of the 1939 blockbuster film: "Frankly, my dear, I don't give a damn."

(In the novel, there is no "frankly.")

Here's how the very long scene plays out at the end of several pages. Rhett has announced that their marriage is over and that he is leaving.

"Stop," she said suddenly. She had hardly heard anything he had said. Certainly her mind had not taken it in. But she knew she could no longer endure with any fortitude the sound of his voice when there was no love in it.

He paused and looked at her quizzically.

"Well, you get my meaning, don't you?" he questioned, rising to his feet.

She threw out her hands to him, palms up, in the age-old gesture of appeal and her heart, again, was in her face.

"No," she cried. "All I know is that you do not love me and you are going away! Oh, my darling, if you go, what shall I do?"

For a moment he hesitated as if debating whether a kind lie were kinder in the long run than the truth. Then he shrugged.

"Scarlett, I was never one to patiently pick up broken fragments and glue them together and tell myself that the mended whole was as good as new. What is broken is broken—and I'd rather remember it as it was at its best then mend it and see the broken places as long as I lived. Perhaps, if I were younger—" he sighed. "But I'm too old to believe in such sentimentalities as clean slates and starting all over. I'm too old to shoulder the burden of constant lies that go with living in polite disillusionment. I couldn't live with you and lie to you and I certainly couldn't lie to myself. I can't even lie to you now. I wish I could care what you do or where you go, but I can't."

He drew a short breath and said lightly but softly:

"My dear, I don't give a damn."

She silently watched him go up the stairs, feeling that she would strangle at the pain in her throat.

She agonizes for a page, then raises her chin and thinks determinedly:

She could get Rhett back. She knew she could. There had never been a man she couldn't get, once she set her mind upon him.

"I'll think of it all tomorrow, at Tara. I can stand it then. Tomorrow, I'll think of some way to get him back. After all, tomorrow is another day."

THE END

It is interesting to note that the producer of the film, David Selznick, was forced to pay a $5,000 fine for breaking "the code" by employing the then-shocking word "damn."

It was also interesting to me upon re-reading the book, a far richer and harder-hitting work than the film, to find that Rhett is a full-blown alcoholic, though under control, and is drunk in nearly every scene, which distresses Scarlett throughout their relationship.

ဆ ❖ ❀

OF ALL THE GREAT WRITERS OF THE TWENTIES AND THIRTIES SCOTT Fitzgerald is the one I'd like to have met. The closest I came was his daughter, Scottie, who roomed with my cousin at Vassar. What would I have asked him? Perhaps, tell me more about what happened to those characters in *Tender is the Night*.

Many people think that F. Scott Fitzgerald's 1934 novel *Tender Is the Night* is at least the equal of his celebrated *The Great Gatsby*. There are many fine scenes in the telling of the marriage of Dr. Dick Diver, his wife Nicole, and the seventeen-year-old actress, Rosemary Hoyt, as they live and flounder in the fledgling summer colony in the south of France circa 1925.

In a touching scene between the doctor and the young woman, she offers herself to the older man.

Her room in the hotel was diagonally across from theirs and nearer the elevator. When they reached the door she said suddenly:

"I know you don't love me—I don't expect it. But you said I should have told you about my birthday. Well, I did, and now for my birthday present I want you to come into my room for a minute while I tell you something. Just one minute."

They went in and he closed the door, and Rosemary stood close to him, not touching him. The night had drawn the color from her face—she was pale as pale now, she was a white carnation left after a dance.

"When you smile—" He had recovered his paternal attitude, perhaps because of Nicole's silent proximity, "I always think I'll see a gap where you've lost some baby teeth."

But he was too late—she came close up against him with a forlorn whisper.

"Take me."

"Take you where?"

Astonishment froze him rigid.

"Go on," she whispered. "Oh, please go on, whatever they do. I don't care if I don't like it—I never expected to—I've always hated to think about it but now I don't. I want you to."

She was astonished at herself—she had never imagined she could talk like that. She was calling on things she had read, seen, dreamed through a decade of convent hours. Suddenly she knew too that it was one of her greatest roles and she flung herself into it more passionately.

"This is not as it should be," Dick deliberated. "Isn't it just the champagne? Let's more or less forget it."

"Oh, no, *now*. I want you to do it now, take me, show me, I'm absolutely yours and I want to be."

"For one thing, have you thought how much it would hurt Nicole?"

"She won't know—this won't have anything to do with her."

He continued kindly.

"Then there's the fact that I love Nicole."

"But you can love more than just one person, can't you? Like I love Mother and I love you—more. I love you more now."

"—In the fourth place you're not in love with me but you might be afterwards, and that would begin your life with a terrible mess."

"No, I promise I'll never see you again. I'll get Mother and go to America right away."

He dismissed this. He was remembering too vividly the youth and freshness of her lips. He took another tone.

"You're just in that mood."

"Oh, please, I don't care even if I had a baby. I could go into Mexico like a girl at the studio. Oh, this is so different from anything I ever thought—I used to hate it when they kissed me seriously." He saw she was still under the impression that it must happen. "Some of them had great big teeth, but you're all different and beautiful. I want you to do it."

"I believe you think people just kiss some way and you want me to kiss you."

"Oh, don't tease me—I'm not a baby. I know you're not in love with me." She was suddenly humble and quiet. "I didn't expect that much. I know I must seem just nothing to you."

"Nonsense. But you seem young to me." His thoughts added, "—there'd be so much to teach you."

Rosemary waited, breathing eagerly till Dick said: "And lastly things aren't arranged so that this could be as you want."

Her face drooped with dismay and disappointment and Dick said automatically. "We'll have to simply—" He stopped himself, followed her to the bed, sat down beside her while she wept. He was suddenly confused, not about the ethics of the matter, for the impossibility of it was sheerly indicated from all angles, but simply confused, and for a moment his usual grace, the tensile strength of his balance, was absent.

"I knew you wouldn't," she sobbed. "It was just a forlorn hope."

He stood up.

"Good night, child. This is a damn shame. Let's drop it out of the picture." He gave her two lines of hospital patter to go to sleep on. "So many people are going to love you and it might be nice to meet your first love all intact, emotionally too. That's an old-fashioned idea, isn't it?" She looked up at him as he took a step toward the door; she looked at him without the slightest idea as to what was in his head, she saw him take another step in slow motion, turn and look at her again, and she wanted for a moment to hold him and devour him, wanted his mouth, his ears, his coat collar, wanted to surround him and engulf him, she saw his hand fall on the doorknob. Then she gave up and sank back on the bed. When the door closed she got up and went to the mirror, where she began brushing her hair, sniffling a little. One hundred and fifty strokes Rosemary gave it, as usual, then a hundred and fifty more. She brushed it until her arm ached, then she changed arms and went on brushing....

What a lovely exchange:

"Take me."
"Take you where?"

Compare that amusing "Take me" with the once enormously popular writer of Westerns, Zane Grey's serious "Take me" in a typically old-fashioned and overwrought passage from one of his dozens of bestsellers:

"I am an outcast. I am hunted. If I made you my wife it might be to your shame and sorrow"..."Take me," she cried, and the soft, deep-toned, passionate voice shook Adam's heart. She would share his wanderings. "Goodbye, Oella," he said huskily. And he strode forth to drive his burro out into the lonely, melancholy desert night.

There are so many stories about Scott Fitzgerald. One was told me by someone who was there:

Fitzgerald and his wife Zelda were in Paris, and he had received the invitation of all invitations: tea time at the aloof Edith Wharton's palatial villa outside the city.

Terribly nervous about meeting the grande dame of letters, the wealthy blueblood author of *House of Mirth*, et cetera, Scott fortified himself at the elegant bar of the Ritz, and then, when Zelda refused to go, he went alone by cab.

He was totally overwhelmed by the sophistication and erudite conversation of the famous guests—the filmmakers and artists and titled gentry—and he finally and suddenly blurted out:

"Yes, but when my wife and I first came here we—we stayed in—in a—*whorehouse*!"

There was a dead silence.

Then Mrs. Wharton said gently, "Well, do go on, Mr. Fitzgerald. Tell us what you did in the whorehouse?"

Fitzgerald fled, went back to the Ritz, put his head down on the bar, beat his fists, and moaned:

"They beat me, they beat me...."

Romance scenes can be important and a pleasure to read. But unless one is reading porn for porn's sake, the romantic scenes should be more than about sex.

There should be more to a love story than just the lovers getting together.

Think of Romeo and Juliet's family feuding and the many other complications that occur in that great love story or, for a more modern example, Graham Greene's marvelous and heart-breaking novel, *The End of the Affair*.

℥ ❧ ℣

ONE OF BROADWAY'S MOST DELICATE SCENES WAS THE TENDER ending of Robert Anderson's play (and film) *Tea and Sympathy* when the boarding school teacher's wife gives herself to the schoolboy who'd wrongly been called a homosexual by his cruel schoolmates. She does it to restore his belief in himself and his manhood, and it is a lovely example of how to leave a scene up to the imagination.

Laura seeing a bolt on the door, slides it to. Then she stands looking at Tom, her hand at her neck. With a slight and delicate movement, she unbuttons the top button of her blouse, and moves toward Tom. When she gets alongside the bed, she reaches out her hand, still keeping one hand at her blouse. Tom makes no move. Just watches her.

Laura makes a little move with the outstretched hand, asking for his hand. TOM slowly moves his hand to hers.

LAURA (Stands there holding his hand and smiling gently at him. Then she sits and looks down at the boy and after a moment, barely audible): And now…nothing?
Tom's other hand comes up and with both his hands he brings her hand to his lips.

LAURA (Smiles tenderly at this gesture, and after a moment): Years from now…when you talk about this…and you will…be kind.

Gently she brings the boy's hands toward her opened blouse, as the lights slowly dim out…and…

THE CURTAIN FALLS

In a rare happening, the three Broadway stars, Deborah Kerr, John Kerr, and Leif Erickson, repeated their parts in the fine 1956 film directed by Vicente Minnelli—and the above scene stayed in the film version.

I once saw Elaine May and Mike Nichols at San Francisco's Hungry I nightclub do a parody of that scene.

Mike, starting to unzip his fly, "Years from now, when you talk about this…and you will…."

Fadeout.

8

Revenge

Pay attention all writers! Injustice stories rarely fail to please the reader (and editors)—that is if the bad guy or guys get their comeuppance in an interesting and credible manner. (See John Grisham's 2005 bestseller, *The Broker*.) Since time immemorial, writers have gravitated to stories where someone is unjustly accused and subsequently avenges the wrong. One of the best, *The Count of Monte Cristo*, written by Alexandre Dumas way back in 1844 was, and remains, an exciting adventure story full of mystery and intrigue.

Edmond Dantès is a young sea captain in the time of Napoleon Bonaparte who is politically framed by four "friends"; on his very wedding day he is arrested and taken to the dread dungeons of the Chateau d'If, an island prison off of Marseilles. After several years there in total isolation, he hears a scraping and realizes there is another prisoner on the other side of the wall. They dig a tunnel little by little and finally get through to each other. It is the Abbé Faria, a brilliant old man, who daily sets about teaching Edmond history, mathematics, and languages. In Edmond's fourteenth year of captivity, the old man falls mortally ill, but not before telling Edmond where to find a vast buried fortune on the island of Monte Cristo should he ever escape.

But how to escape? The old man dies and the guards put him into a sack awaiting burial; this scene follows:

> "Ah, ah!" he muttered, "where's this idea coming from? God! From God! None but the dead get out of this dungeon, the place of the dead!"
>
> Without giving himself time to reconsider his decision,

he bent over the appalling sack and opened it with the knife that Abbé Faria had made. He lifted the corpse from the sack and dragged it into the tunnel to his own cell. He laid it on his cot, wrapped around its head the rag he wore at night round his own, covered it with the bedspread, once again kissed the ice-cold brow, and trying vainly to avoid the eyes which glared horribly, turned the head towards the wall so that the jailer might, when he brought his evening meal, think that he was asleep, as was his frequent custom. He returned to the other cell, took from the hiding-place the needle and thread, flung off his rags so that they'd feel naked flesh only beneath the coarse sack-cloth, and getting inside the sack, he placed himself in the same position in which the dead man had been laid, and sewed up the mouth of the sack on the inside. The beating of his heart might have been heard, if by any mischance they had entered at that moment.

Later the guards come for the body.

The door opened, and a dim light reached Dantès's eyes through the sack that covered him. He saw two shadows walking towards his bed, a third remaining at the door with a torch in his hand. The two men approached the bed and grabbed the sack by its ends.

"Sure heavy for a thin old man," said one, as he lifted his end.

Edmond doesn't know where he is being taken but he soon finds out after suddenly feeling himself thrown into the air.

Dantès had been flung into the sea, into whose depths he was drawn down and down by a thirty-six-pound shot tied to his feet.

The sea is the cemetery of Chateau d'If.

Edmond cuts himself out of the sack and fights to the surface. He is subsequently picked up by a ship of smugglers, finds the fortune on the island, re-styles himself as the rich and debonair Count of Monte Cristo, and proceeds to seek out and destroy in different ways the unsuspecting bad guys who had put him in prison.

The writing is amazingly terse and graphic and modern, considering the age of the novel.

The story has been the inspiration for plays and films, the most successful being the 1934 movie with Robert Donat as Edmond and O. P. Heggie as Abbé Faria.

ಔ ❖ ಛ

ROALD DAHL'S MALICIOUS SHORT STORY, "NUNC DIMITTIS" (which I translate as "Now Get Lost") is as *noir* as any story ever written.

Dilettante Lionel Lampson is a high society old bore who thinks his favorite dinner companion, Janet de Pelagia, adores him. When he finds out that Janet, a pillar of society, secretly despises him and makes fun of him behind his back, he vows revenge.

He has learned that the most famous portrait painter of women in England has a novel way of approaching a portrait; he first paints the ladies nude, then in the next session adds the underclothes, and finally the dress. Lionel commissions the man to paint Janet life size and full length, and she is pleased with the overly flattering result which hides her corseted fat, sagging breasts and bow legs. Then secretly, Lionel removes the two top layers of paint to reveal the underpainting of the ugly unclothed woman.

He then invites the cream of London society to a gala candlelight dinner. At the climax of the evening, the bright lights go on and reveal to all the devastating painting.

> They all screwed up their eyes, opened them again, gazed about them.
>
> At that point I got up from my chair and slid quietly from the room, but as I went I saw a sight that I shall never forget as long as I live. It was Janet, with both hands in mid-air, stopped, frozen rigid, caught in the act of gesticulating toward someone across the table. Her mouth had dropped open two inches and she wore the surprised, not-quite-understanding look of a person who precisely one second before has been shot dead right through the heart.

In the hall outside I paused and listened to the beginning of the uproar, the shrill cries of the ladies and the outraged unbelieving exclamations of the men; and soon there was a great hum of noise with everybody talking or shouting at the same time. Then—and this was the sweetest moment of all—I heard Lord Mulherrin's voice, roaring above the rest, "Here! Someone! Hurry! Give her some water quick!"

Lionel goes away for a while, surprised and crushed that all his old friends now hate him.

> 66 Since time immemorial, writers have gravitated to stories where someone is unjustly accused and subsequently avenges the wrong. 99

Then at noon today came the final crushing blow. The post arrived, and with it—I can hardly bring myself to write about it, I am so ashamed—came a letter, the sweetest, most tender little note imaginable from none other than Janet de Pelagia herself. She forgave me completely, she wrote, for everything I had done. She knew it was only a joke and I must not listen to the horrid things other people were saying about me. She loved me as she always had and always would to her dying day.

Oh, what a cad, what a brute I felt when I read this! The more so when I found that she had actually sent me by the same post a small present as an added sign of her affection—a half pound jar of my favorite food of all, fresh caviar.

I can never under any circumstances resist good caviar. It is perhaps my greatest weakness. So although I naturally had no appetite whatsoever for food at dinner-time this evening, I must confess I took a few spoonfuls of the stuff in an effort to console myself in my misery. It is even possible that I took a shade too much, because I haven't been feeling any too chipper this last hour or so. Perhaps I ought to go up right away and get myself some bicarbonate of soda. I can easily come back and finish this later, when I'm in better trim.

You know—now I come to think of it, I really do feel rather ill all of a sudden.

₧ ❖ ‑

IT'S HARD TO KNOW EXACTLY WHY PADDY CHAYEFSKY'S 1976 FILM, *Network*, starring Peter Finch as the overwrought TV personality Howard Beale made such an impact. For some time people went around saying, "I'm mad as hell and I'm not going to take it anymore!"

They still do.

> *On the SHOW MONITOR the footage flicks to Sheikh Zaki Yamani being interviewed by a corps of correspondents.*

FLETCHER (*voice-off*): Saudi Arabian oil minister Sheikh Zaki Yamani flew to London yesterday for further consultations with his government. He returned to the Vienna meetings today....

> *Nobody in the control room is paying attention to Yamani. They are watching the double bank of black-and-white monitors showing Howard Beale entering the studio, drenched, hunched, staring into his own space, and moving with singled-minded purpose across the studio past cameras and CREW to his desk, which is being vacated for him by Jack Snowden. The film clips of Yamani ends.*

ASSISTANT DIRECTOR: Ready...two...

DIRECTOR: Take two.

> *And suddenly the obsessed face of Howard Beale with unworldly fervor and red eyes, manifestly mad, fills the MONITOR SCREEN.*

HOWARD (*on monitor*): I don't have to tell you things are bad. Everybody knows things are bad. It's a depression. Everybody's out of work or scared of losing their job, the dollar buys a nickel's worth, banks are going bust, shop-keepers keep a gun under the counter, punks are running wild in the streets, and there's nobody anywhere who seems to know what to do, and there's no end to it. We know the air's unfit to breathe and our food is unfit to eat, and we sit and watch our teevees while some local newscaster tells us today we had fifteen homicides and sixty-three violent crimes, as if that's the way it's supposed to be. We all know things are bad. Worse than bad. They're crazy. It's like everything's going crazy. So we don't go out anymore. We sit in the house, and slowly the world we live in gets smaller, and all we ask is, please, at least leave us alone in our own living rooms. Let me have my toaster and my teevee and my hair dryer and my steel-belted radials, and I won't say anything, just leave us alone. Well, I'm not going to leave you alone. I want you to get mad.

ANOTHER ANGLE showing the rapt attention of the PEOPLE in the control room, especially of Diana.

HOWARD: I don't want you to protest. I don't want you to riot. I don't want you to write your congressmen. Be-cause I wouldn't know what to tell you to write. I don't know what to do about the depression and the inflation and the defense budget and the Russians and crime in the street. All I know is first you've got to get mad. You've got to say, "I'm a human being, goddammit. My life has value." So I want you to get up now. I want you to get out of your chairs and go to the window. Right now. I want you to go to the window, open it, and stick your head out and yell. I want you to yell, "I'm mad as hell, and I'm not going to take this any more!"

DIANA (*grabs Hunter's shoulder*): How many stations does this go out live to?

HUNTER: Sixty-seven. I know it goes to Louisville and At-lanta, I think…

HOWARD (*on monitor*): Get up from your chairs. Go to the window. Open it. Stick your head out and yell and keep yelling.

Diana has already left the control room.

೫ ❖ ೞ

STORIES THAT DEPEND ENTIRELY UPON THE FINAL SCENE OR PARAGRAPH have gone out of fashion since O. Henry's gimmicky tales, Frank Stockton's "The Lady or the Tiger," or Saki's (H. H. Munro) weird stories, but here is one that stands up because the emphasis is on character.

Frederick Forsyth is a master of the suspense scene, witness those in his best sellers *The Day of the Jackal*, *The Odessa File*, *The Dogs of War*, et alia.

He is also a great short story writer. One of his most romantic—and shocking—is his 1982 "No Comebacks."

It begins this way.

> Mark Sanderson liked women. For that matter he also liked Aberdeen Angus fillet steaks, medium rare with tossed heart-of-lettuce salad, and he consumed both with equal if passing enjoyment. If he ever felt a little puckish, he rang up the appropriate supplier and ordered what he needed to be sent round to his penthouse. He could afford it, for he was a millionaire several times over, and that was in pounds sterling, which even in these troubled times are worth about two U.S. dollars.

Mark callously takes women and then tosses them aside like used Kleenex. But then, at thirty-six, he meets Angela Summers, a very proper and intelligent woman married to a retired Army major and living in the south of Spain. For the first time in his life he falls desperately and totally in love, and they see each other for an intense week.

> "A week is not long to have an affair but it can be enough to change a life, or two, or even three."

Mark is obsessed; here is the only thing in the world that he has ever wanted that he can't have.

He proposed to her that she leave her husband, divorce him and that they marry. Because he was evidently very serious she took the suggestion seriously, and shook her head.

"I couldn't do that," she said.

"I love you. Not just passingly, but absolutely and completely. I'd do anything for you."

She gazed forward through the windscreen at the darkened street. "Yes, I think you do, Mark. We shouldn't have gone this far. I should have noticed earlier and stopped seeing you."

"Do you love me? Even a little?"

"It's too early to say. I can't be rushed like that."

"But could you love me? Now or ever?"

Again she had the womanly sense to take the question completely seriously.

"I think I could. Or rather, could *have* loved you. You're not anything like you and your reputation try to make you out to be. Underneath all the cynicism you're really rather vulnerable, and that's nice."

"Then leave him and marry me."

"I can't do that. I'm married to Archie and I can't leave him."

Sanderson felt a surge of anger at the faceless man in Spain who stood in his way. "What's he got that I can't offer you?"

She smiled a trifle ruefully. "Oh, nothing. He's really rather weak, and not very effectual..."

"Then why not leave him?"

"Because he needs me," she said simply.

"I need you."

She shook her head. "No, not really. You want me, but you can get by without me. He can't. He just hasn't the strength."

"It's not just that I want you, Angela. I love you, more than anything else that's every happened to me. I adore you, and I desire you."

"You don't understand," she said after a pause. "Women love to be loved and adore to be adored. They desire to be desired, but more than all these together a woman needs to be needed. And Archie needs me, like the air he breathes."

Sanderson ground his Sobranie into the ashtray.

"So, with him you stay…'until death us do part,'" he grated.

She didn't rise to the mockery but nodded and turned to stare at him. "Yes, that's about it. Till death us do part. I'm sorry, Mark, but that's the way I am. In another time and another place, and if I weren't married to Archie, it might have been different, probably would. But I am married to my husband, and that's the end of it."

The following day she was gone. He had his chauffeur drive her to the airport to catch the Valencia plane.

Mark is in agony. The phrase "until death us do part" keeps echoing in his brain. He loves this woman with all his being, and he must have her at any cost. He realizes there is only one way—the major must die.

With Mark's money it is not too difficult to hire an assassin, a Corsican, who agrees to do it for five thousand pounds.

And here is the final chilling scene.

The two men met the next evening in the bar in the Rue Miollin, the killer and the client. Calvi had telephoned his message that morning after arriving back from Valencia the previous evening just before midnight, and Sanderson had flown over at once. The client seemed nervous as he handed over the rest of the £5000.

"No problems at all?" he asked again. The Corsican smiled quietly and shook his head.

"Very simple, and your major is very dead. Two bullets in the heart and one through the head."

"No one saw you?" asked the Englishman. "No witnesses?"

"No." The Corsican rose, patting the wads of notes into his breast pocket. "Though I'm afraid I was interrupted at the end. For some reason it was raining hard, and someone came in and saw me with the body."

The Englishman stared at him in horror. "Who?"

"A woman."

"Tall, dark-haired?"

"Yeah. A nice-looking piece too." He looked down at the expression of panic in the client's face, and patted the man on the shoulder.

"Don't worry, monsieur," he said reassuringly, "there will be no comebacks. I shot her, too."

This is what editors call a "biter-gets-bit" story—in other words, a character who does a bad thing in the beginning of the story gets his or her comeuppance at the end.

છ ❖ ભ

ROALD DAHL'S "LAMB TO SLAUGHTER" MIGHT BE TERMED THE ultimate in gallows humor.

Mary Malloy is six months pregnant, a good and faithful wife, and happily married, she thinks, to Pat, a police detective. Then one evening he comes home and summarily announces that he's leaving her, presumably for another woman.

She had been preparing dinner and, stunned, she dazedly continues, taking a leg of lamb from the freezer.

A leg of lamb.

All right then, they would have lamb for supper. She carried it upstairs, holding the thing bone-end of it with both of her hands, and as she went through the living-room, she saw him standing over by the window with his back to her, and she stopped.

"For God's sake," he said, hearing her, but not turning round. "Don't make supper for me. I'm going out."

At that point, Mary Maloney simply walked up behind him and without any pause she swung the big frozen leg of lamb high in the air and brought it down as hard as she could on the back of his head.

She might just as well have hit him with a steel club.

She stepped back a pace, waiting, and the funny thing was that he remained standing there for at least four or five seconds, gently swaying. Then he crashed to the carpet.

The violence of the crash, the noise, the small table over-turning, helped bring her out of the shock. She came out slowly, feeling cold and surprised, and she stood for a while blinking at the body, still holding the ridiculous piece of meat tight with both hands.

All right, she told herself. So I've killed him.

Mechanically, she puts the leg of lamb in the oven. She establishes an alibi for herself, then calls the cops, her husband's friends, and tear-fully tells them she came back from the store to find Pat bludgeoned.

They come over to investigate, commiserate, and take the body away. She invites them to have the dinner she was preparing for dear Pat. They love the leg of lamb and dig into it. The final scene as they are eating it:

"That's a hell of a big club the guy must've used to hit poor Patrick," one of them was saying. "The doc says his skull was smashed all to pieces just like from a sledgehammer."

"That's why it ought to be easy to find."

"Exactly what I say."

"Whoever done it, they're not going to be carrying a thing like that around with them longer than they need."

One of them belched.

"Personally, I think it's right here on the premises."

"Probably right under our very noses. What you think, Jack?"

And in the other room, Mary Maloney began to giggle.

9

Betrayal

T HERE'S A SAYING THAT THE HOLLYWOOD SCREENWRITER IS TREATED like a hooker who has been used, paid, and is hanging around in the hopes of getting breakfast. Also often quoted is the great producer Irving Thalberg's line: "The most important person in Hollywood is the writer, but don't tell the sonsofbitches."

Budd Schulberg was determined to break the mold with his 1954 screenplay of *On the Waterfront*. The agreement with director Elia Kazan was that not a word of his screenplay could be changed without his consent. Turned down by all the major studios, it was finally produced by Sam Spiegel and won eight Oscars, including Best Picture, Best Actor (Marlon Brando), and Best Supporting Actress (Eva Marie Saint), and, of course, Best Screenplay.

Everyone remembers one line from the great film. Here is the scene that builds up to it:

Brando, a washed-up prize fighter working as a stevedore on the corrupt docks of New York, is in a cab with his brother Charley (Rod Steiger). Charley is a big shot crook in the mob who controls the waterfront, and he fears that his brother will testify against the organized rampant crime. Charley tries to bribe him.

CHARLEY: There's a slot for a boss loader on the new pier
we're opening up.

TERRY (interested): Boss loader!

CHARLEY: Ten cents a hundred pounds on everything that

moves in and out. And you don't have to lift a finger. It'll be three-four hundred a week just for openers.

TERRY: And for all that dough I don't do nothin'?

CHARLEY: Absolutely nothing. You do nothing and you say nothing. You understand, don't you, kid?

TERRY (struggling with an unfamiliar problem of conscience and loyalties): Yeah—yeah—I guess I do—but there's a lot more to this whole thing than I thought, Charley.

CHARLEY: You don't mean you're thinking of testifying against—(turns a thumb in toward himself)

TERRY: I don't know—I don't know! I tell you I ain't made up my mind yet. That's what I wanted to talk to you about.

CHARLEY (patiently, as to a stubborn child). Listen, Terry, these piers we handle through the local—you know what they're worth to us?

TERRY: I know. I know.

CHARLEY: Well, then, you know Cousin Johnny isn't going to jeopardize a setup like that for one rubber-lipped...

TERRY (simultaneous): Don't say that!

CHARLEY (continuing): —ex-tanker who's walking on his heels?

TERRY: Don't say that!

CHARLEY: What the hell!!!

TERRY: I could have been better!

CHARLEY: Listen, that isn't the point.

TERRY: I could have been better!

CHARLEY: The point is—there isn't much time, kid.

There is a painful pause, as they appraise each other.

TERRY (desperately): I tell you, Charley, I haven't made up
my mind!

CHARLEY: Make up your mind, kid, I beg you, before we get
to four thirty-seven River....

TERRY (stunned): Four thirty-seven – that isn't where Gerry
G...?

Charley nods solemnly. Terry grows more agitated.

TERRY: Charley...you wouldn't take me to Gerry G...?

*Charley continues looking at him. He does not deny it.
They stare at each other for a moment. Then suddenly
Terry starts out of the cab. Charley pulls a pistol. Terry is
motionless, now, looking at Charley.*

CHARLEY: Take the boss loading, kid. For God's sake. I don't
want to hurt you.

TERRY (hushed, gently guiding the gun down toward Charley's
lap): Charley...Charley...Wow....

CHARLEY (genuinely): I wish I didn't have to do this, Terry.

*Terry eyes him, beaten. Charley leans back and looks at
Terry strangely. Terry raises his hands above his head,
somewhat in the manner of a prizefighter mitting the
crowd. The image nicks Charley's memory.*

TERRY (an accusing sigh): Wow....

CHARLEY (gently): What do you weigh these days, slugger?

TERRY (shrugs): —eighty-seven, eighty-eight. What's it to you?

CHARLEY (nostalgically): Gee, when you tipped one seventy-five you were beautiful. You should've been another Billy Conn. That skunk I got to manage you brought you along too fast.

TERRY: It wasn't him! (years of abuse crying out in him) It was you, Charley. You and Johnny. Like the night the two of youse come in the dressing room and says, 'Kid, this ain't your night—we're going for the price on Wilson.' *It ain't my night.* I'd of taken Wilson apart that night! I was ready—remember the early rounds throwing them combinations. So what happens—This bum Wilson he gets the title shot—outdoors in the ball park!—and what do I get—a couple of bucks and a one-way ticket to Palookaville. (more and more aroused as he relives it) It was you, Charley. You was my brother. You should of looked out for me. Instead of making me take them dives for the short-end money.

CHARLEY (defensively): I always had a bet down for you. You saw some money.

TERRY (agonized): See! You don't understand!

CHARLEY: I tried to keep you in good with Johnny.

TERRY: You don't understand! I could've been a contender. I could've had class and been somebody. Real class. Instead of a bum, let's face it, which is what I am. It was you, Charley.

Charley takes a long, fond look at Terry. Then he glances quickly out the window.

MEDIUM SHOT. WATERFRONT. NIGHT.

From Charley's angle. A gloomy light reflects the street numbers—433—435

INT. CLOSE. CAB. ON CHARLEY AND TERRY. NIGHT.

TERRY: It was you, Charley....

CHARLEY (turning back to Terry, his tone suddenly changed): Okay—I'll tell him I couldn't bring you in. Ten to one they won't believe it, but—go ahead, blow. Jump out, quick, and keep going...and God help you from here on in.

By letting Terry off the hook, Charley has signed his own death warrant. Sometime later a voice calls to Terry outside of his apartment to come down if he wants to see Charley. Terry and his girl, Edie, go down looking for Charley.

SAME VOICE IN FOG: Wanna see Charley? He's over here.

TERRY (as they hurry forward): Hey, Charley....

EXT. MEDIUM CLOSE. WHITE WALL. NIGHT.

The headlights of a car suddenly illuminate Charley against the wall. Charley is leaning against the lamp post, in a very casual attitude, looking as dapper as usual. Terry and Edie run to him. The car drives off.

TERRY: Looking for me, Charley?

Charley seems to study them silently. Terry nudges him.

TERRY: Hey, Charley.

Charley slides down the wall and crumples to the ground. Dead. Edie screams. Terry drops beside the body.

TERRY: He's dead. He's dead. Those scummy, good-for-nuthin' butchers….

Subsequently, Terry hunts down the evil boss, beats him up, but in turn is beaten badly by the goons. But his actions rally the stevedores to throw off the shackles of the mob, and the ending is upbeat.

Brando's performance is one of his finest, but it wasn't easy making him stick to the script. Budd Schulberg told me recently that the actor kept trying to "improve" the lines. ("Listen, Marlon, it's 'contenduh'! Not 'champeen' or 'big-shot'!")

Marlon insisted on leaving the set every day exactly at 4:00 to see his psychiatrist, so the final two-shots of Charley and Terry in the taxi cab scene were done without Marlon even being present and with Elia Kazan feeding Steiger Brando's lines.

"Steiger never got over it," Schulberg chuckles. "It was one of the last things he complained about just before he died."

A literary anecdotal lagniappe, speaking of author Budd Schulberg:

As the young author of the huge best-seller, *What Makes Sammy Run*, Schulberg was wined and dined in Europe. At a cocktail party on the Riviera, someone said to the legendary novelist Somerset Maugham, who had suffered from stuttering all his life, "let me introduce you to the new young American writer."

Shy, and also a life-time stutterer, Schulberg, extended his hand and said:

"I'm h-h-honored, Mister M-M-Maugham."

The great author turned away, saying, "Who, exactly, is that in-in-insolent p-p-puppy?!"

෨ ❖ ୣ

ONE OF THE MOST MOVING SCENES IN ALL MARK TWAIN'S WRITING IS the one from *Huckleberry Finn* where Huck berates himself for not turning in Jim, the runaway slave. The boy is such a brainwashed Southerner that he cannot see that he truly loves his black friend.

They are on the raft, wanting to get to the town of Cairo, where Jim can feel safe at last.

> There warn't nothing to do, now, but to look out sharp for the town, and not pass it without seeing it. He said he'd be mighty sure to see it, because he'd be a free man the minute he seen it, but if he missed it he'd be in the slave country again and no more show for freedom. Every little while he jumps up and says:
>
> 'Dah she is!'
>
> But it warn't. It was Jack-o-lanterns, or lightning-bugs; so he set down again, and went to watching, same as before. Jim said it made him all over trembly and feverish to be so close to freedom. Well, I can tell you it made me all over trembly and feverish, too, to hear him, because I begun to get it through my head that he *was* most free—and who was to blame for it? Why, *me*. I couldn't get that out of my conscience, no how nor no way. It got to troubling me so I couldn't rest; I couldn't stay still in one place. It hadn't ever come home to me before, what this thing was that I was doing. But now it did; and it staid with me, and scorched me more and more. I tried to make out to myself that *I* warn't to blame, because *I* didn't run Jim off from his rightful owner; but it warn't no use, conscience up and says, every time, 'But you knowed he was running for his freedom, and you could a paddled ashore and told somebody.' That was so—I couldn't get around that, noway. That was where it pinched. Conscience says to me, 'What had poor Miss Watson done to you, that you could see her nigger go off right under your eyes and never say one single word? What did that poor old woman do to you, that you could treat her so mean Why, she tried to learn you your book, she tried to learn you your manners, she tried to be good to you every way she knowed how. *That's* what she done.'

The reader, of course, is saying to himself, "Huck, you got it all wrong."

Jim talked out loud all the time while I was talking to myself. He was saying how the first thing he would do when he got to a free State he would go to saving up money and never spend a single cent, and when he got enough he would buy his wife, which was owned on a farm close to where Miss Watson lived; and then they would both work to buy the two children, and if their master wouldn't sell them, they'd get an Ab'litionist to go and steal them.

It most froze me to hear such talk. He wouldn't ever dared to talk such talk in his life before. Just see what a difference it made in him the minute he judged he was about free. It was according to the old saying, 'give a nigger an inch and he'll take an ell.' Thinks I, this is what comes of my not thinking. Here was this nigger which I had as good as helped to run away, coming right out flat-footed and saying he would steal his chil-dren—children that belonged to a man I didn't even know; a man that hadn't ever done me no harm.

Huck decides to paddle to shore and turn the unsuspecting Jim in.

He jumped and got the canoe ready, and put his old coat in the bottom for me to set on, and give me the paddle; and as I shoved off, he says:

'Pooty soon I'll be a-shout'n for joy, en I'll say, it's all on accounts o'Huck; I's a free man, en I couldn't ever ben free ef it hadn' been for Huck; Huck done it. Jim won't ever forgit you, Huck; you's de bes' fren' Jim's ever had; en you's de *only* fren' old Jim's got now.'

I was paddling off, all in a sweat to tell on him; but when he says this, it seemed to kind of take the tuck all out of me. I went along slow then, and I warn't right down certain whether I was glad I started or whether I warn't. When I was fifty yards off, Jim says:

'Dah you goes, de ole true Huck; de on'y white genlman dat ever kep' his promise to ole Jim.'

Well, I just felt sick. But I says, I *got* to do it—I can't get *out* of it.

But, of course, Huck does the right thing in the end.

Betrayal as a theme for writers, like injustice, has been around for a long and highly successful period of time, from Homer's *Iliad* to Judas Escariot to The *Count of Monte Cristo* to *The Godfather* to *The Da Vinci Code*, and hundreds of plots in between. It seems to be most effective and moving when the reader sees the betrayal coming and the protagonist doesn't.

Betrayal has often served well books by such best-selling authors as Elmore Leonard, Ed McBain, Harlan Coben, and Michael Connelly.

10

Humor

––––––

FEW COMEDIES HAVE HAD THE LONG LIFE AND BEEN SEEN IN SUCH varied mediums as Neil Simon's *The Odd Couple* since it first arrived on Broadway in 1965. Oscar Madison, who is divorced, has reached the end of his tether with persnickety roommate Felix Ungar, separated from his wife. (Walter Matthau played Oscar in both the stage and film version; Art Carney was the stage Felix, Jack Lemmon the film Felix.)

Why has it been, and remained, so successful?

First, it's about likeable people with a big problem.

Second, it is a human, understandable problem: two very different people trying to live under the same roof. The humor comes out of everyday, familiar, domestic situations, almost like a marriage. The only difference being that the problems occur between two heterosexual men rather than a man and a woman.

Third, there is conflict on every page.

Perhaps the biggest laugh in the whole play comes at the beginning of the third act.

OSCAR: Stay out of there! Stay out of my room!

(He chases after him. Felix dodges around the table as Oscar blocks the hallway.)

FELIX (*Backing away, keeping the table between them*): Watch yourself! Just watch yourself, Oscar!

OSCAR (*With a pointing finger*): I'm warning you. You want

to live here, I don't want to see you, I don't want to hear you and I don't want to smell your cooking. Now get this spaghetti off my poker table.

FELIX: Ha! Ha, ha!

OSCAR: What the hell's so funny?

FELIX: It's not spaghetti. It's linguini!

(Oscar picks up the plate of linguini, crosses to the doorway and hurls it into the kitchen)

OSCAR: Now it's garbage! (*He paces by the couch*)

FELIX (*Looks at Oscar unbelievingly; what an insane thing to do*): You are crazy! I'm a neurotic nut but *you are crazy*!

OSCAR: *I'm* crazy, heh? That's really funny coming from a fruitcake like you.

FELIX (*Goes to the kitchen door and looks in at the mess. Turns back to Oscar*): I'm not cleaning that up.

OSCAR: Is that a promise?

FELIX: Did you hear what I said? I'm not cleaning it up. It's your mess. (*Looking into the kitchen again*) Look at it. Hanging all over the walls.

OSCAR (*Crosses to the landing and looks in the kitchen door*): I like it. (*He closes the door and paces around*)

FELIX (*Fumes*): You'd just let it lie there, wouldn't you? Until it turns hard and brown and...Yich, it's disgusting. I'm cleaning it up. (*He goes into the kitchen. Oscar chases after him. There is the sound of a struggle and falling pots*)

OSCAR: *Leave it alone!* You touch one strand of that linguini—
and I'm gonna punch you right in your sinuses.

FELIX (*Dashes out of the kitchen with Oscar in pursuit. He
stops and tries to calm Oscar down*): Oscar, I'd like you
to take a couple of phenobarbital.

OSCAR (*Points*): Go to your room! Did you hear what I said?
Go to your room!

FELIX: All right, let's everybody just settle down, heh? (*He
puts his hand on Oscar's shoulder to calm him but Oscar
pulls away violently from his touch*)

OSCAR: If you want to live through this night, you'd better tie
me up and lock your doors and windows.

FELIX (*Sits at the table with a great pretense of calm*): All
right, Oscar, I'd like to know what's happened?

OSCAR (*Moves toward him*): What's *happened*?

FELIX (*Hurriedly slides over to the next chair*): That's right.
Something must have caused you to go off the deep end
like this. What is it? Something I said? Something I did?
Heh? What?

OSCAR (*Pacing*): It's nothing you said. It's nothing you did.
It's *you*!

FELIX: I see. Well, that's plain enough.

OSCAR: I could make it plainer but I don't want to hurt you.

FELIX: What is it, the cooking? The cleaning? The crying?

OSCAR (*Moving toward him*): I'll tell you exactly what it is.
It's the cooking, cleaning and crying. It's the talking in

119

your sleep, it's the moose calls that open your ears at two o'clock in the morning. I can't take it any more, Felix. I'm crackin' up. Everything you do irritates me. And when you're not here, the things I know you're gonna do when you come in irritate me. You leave me little notes on my pillow. I told you a hundred times, I can't stand little notes on my pillow. "We're all out of Corn Flakes. F.U." It took me three hours to figure out that F.U. was Felix Ungar. It's not your fault, Felix. It's a rotten combination.

FELIX: I get the picture.

OSCAR: That's just the frame. The picture I haven't even painted yet.

In 1997 I asked Neil Simon about that scene and accused him of naming his character just so he could use those initials. He wrote back:

"No, I swear, I did not write Felix Ungar just for the F.U. joke. Felix had to write Oscar a letter and I tried all different signatures for him. Felee, Ma Ungar, Ungar, Your Roommate, and finally just his initials, F.U.

"I stared at the page in the typewriter and realized I had just stumbled into a goldmine. It's one of those things that probably happen once in your career."

He later let me in on a tip—a good one for any would-be playwright:

"If ever you want to get an audience's full attention, get them hushed and expectantly leaning forward in their seats, have one character say to the other, 'I've never told this to anyone else in the world!'"

No one seems to have come up with a definition of humor or what makes something funny. Neil Simon has a scene in his 1973 play, *The Sunshine Boys*, which tries. Ben is trying to get his old washed up comedian Uncle Willie to go back with his ex-partner, the other Sunshine Boy.

BEN: For the Frito-Lays potato chips. I sent you over to the studio, you couldn't even remember the address.

WILLIE: Don't tell me I didn't remember the lines. The lines

I remembered beautifully. The name of the potato chip I couldn't remember…What was it?

BEN: Frito-Lays.

WILLIE: Say it again.

BEN: Frito-Lays.

WILLIE: I still can't remember it—because it's not funny. If it's funny, I remember it. Alka-Seltzer is funny. You say "Alka-Seltzer," you get a laugh. The other word is not funny. What is it?

BEN: Frito-Lays.

WILLIE: Maybe in *Mexico* that's funny, not here. Fifty-seven years I'm in this business, you learn a few things. You know what makes an audience laugh. Do you know which words are funny and which words are *not* funny?

BEN: You told me a hundred times, Uncle Willie. Words with a "K" in it are funny.

WILLIE: Words with a "K" in it are funny. You didn't know that, did you? If it doesn't have a "K," it's not funny. I'll tell you which words always get a laugh. (*He is about to count on his fingers*)

BEN: Chicken.

WILLIE: Chicken is funny.

BEN: Pickle.

WILLIE: Pickle is funny.

BEN: Cupcake.

WILLIE: Cupcake is funny…Tomato is *not* funny. Roast beef is *not* funny.

BEN: But cookie is funny.

WILLIE: But cookie is funny.

BEN: Uncle Willie, you've explained that to me ever since I was a little boy.

WILLIE: Cucumber is funny.

BEN (*Falling in again*): Car keys.

WILLIE: Car keys is funny.

BEN: Cleveland.

WILLIE: Cleveland is funny…Maryland is *not* funny.

Conflict

I once heard Neil Simon interviewed on TV. The interviewer asked him what the most important element in a play was.

"Conflict," replied Simon.

"Even in the love scenes?"

"*Especially* in the love scenes!" Simon replied.

Simon's *The Odd Couple* wore so well because of the constant conflict; the author never lets up, never lets the audience off the hook. Conflict takes many forms; it doesn't necessarily involve physical conflict, though Oscar and Felix come close to that. Personal conflicts are often more interesting than say, a sword fight or an attack on the Alamo.

Take this excerpt from a scene from Patricia Cornwell's novel, *Cruel and Unusual*. Kay Scarpetta, Cornwell's forensic expert heroine, seems to always be at odds with her devoted but crotchety sidekick, Marino, when solving murders.

"Doc"—Marino met my eyes—"you are driven compared to *anyone*, and most people can't figure you out. You don't exactly walk around with your heart on your sleeve. In fact, you can come across as someone who don't have feelings. You're so damn hard to read that to others who don't know you, it sometimes appears that nothing gets to you. Other cops, lawyers, they ask me about you. They want to know what you're really like, how you can do what you do every day—what the deal is. They see you as somebody who don't get close to anyone."

"And what do you tell them when they ask?" I said.

"I don't tell them a damn thing."

"Are you finished psychoanalyzing me yet, Marino?"

He lit a cigarette. "Look, I'm going to say something to you, and you ain't gonna like it. You've always been this reserved, professional lady—someone real slow to let anybody in, but once the person's there, he's there. He's got a damn friend for life and you'd do anything for him. But you've been different this past year. You've had about a hundred walls up ever since Mark got killed. For those of us around you, it's like being in a room that was once seventy degrees and suddenly the temperature's down to about fifty-five. I don't think you're even aware of it.

(Mark was the love of her life.)

"Might we converse without speaking in clichés, at least for a minute or two?"

"Hey, I can say it in Portuguese or Chinese and you're not going to listen to me."

"If you speak Portuguese or Chinese, I promise I'll listen. In fact, if you ever decide to speak English I promise I'll listen."

"Comments like that don't win you any fans. That's just what I'm talking about."

> "I said it with a smile."
>
> "I've seen you cut open bodies with a smile."
>
> "Sometimes there isn't a difference between the two. I've seen your smile make defense attorneys bleed."
>
> There is a tension here in this small and not-very-amiable scene.
>
> ## Amiability is the enemy of the writer of fiction.
>
> So much more is garnered for the reader in the scene, plot-wise and characterization-wise, by its dialogue being abrasive rather than pleasant.
>
> ## Conflict makes dialogue zing.

℘ ❖ ℜ

So OFTEN COMEDY SCENES ONCE CONSIDERED HILARIOUS (HAROLD Lloyd hanging from the hands of the huge clock, Charlie Chaplin and the edible shoes, Laurel and Hardy moving the piano, etc.) strike us today as mildly risible, perhaps, but from another planet and another era.

James Thurber's humorous writing appears to have fared better than most the vicious vicissitudes of time.

In his most famous work, "The Secret Life of Walter Mitty," a short story, his wimpy protagonist is married to a terrible harridan and he takes refuge in many daydreams in which he is always a stalwart hero, a brilliant surgeon, a fearless aviator or brave, wounded doughboy. ("Set the bones myself, sir.") Here, while waiting in a hotel lobby for his shopping wife, he is transported to a scene in war-torn France:

> There was a rending of wood and splinters flew through the room. "A bit of a near thing," said Captain Mitty carelessly. "The box barrage is closing in," said the sergeant. "We only live once, Sergeant," said Mitty, with his faint, fleeting smile. "Or do we?" He poured another brandy and tossed it off. "I never

seen a man could hold his brandy like you, sir," said the sergeant. "Begging your pardon, sir." Captain Mitty stood up and strapped on his huge Webley-Vickers automatic. "It's forty kilometers through hell, sir," said the sergeant. Mitty finished one last brandy. "After all," he said softy, "what isn't?" The pounding of the cannon increased; there was the rat-tat-tatting of machine guns, and from somewhere came the menacing pocketa-pocketa-pocketa of the new flame-throwers. Walter Mitty walked to the door of the dug-out humming "Auprès de Ma Blonde." He turned and waved to the sergeant. "Cheerio!" he said....

Something struck his shoulder. "I've been looking all over this hotel for you," said Mrs. Mitty. "Why do you have to hide in this old chair? How did you expect me to find you?" "Things close in," said Walter Mitty vaguely. "What?" Mrs. Mitty said. "Did you get the what's-its-name? The puppy biscuit? What's in that box?" "Overshoes," said Mitty. "Couldn't you have put them on in the store?" "I was thinking," said Walter Mitty. "Does it ever occur to you that I am sometimes thinking?" She looked at him. "I'm going to take your temperature when I get you home," she said.

The basis of the story became a formulaic comedy film for Danny Kaye in 1947. But it is a deft depiction of a character's inner thoughts, daydreams, and shows how trapped Mr. Mitty is by his controlling wife.

℘ ❖ ℆

IT HAS BEEN SAID THAT THE BEST WRITERS ARE THE ONES WHO CAN make the most unbelievable stories *believable*.

Pay attention, would-be authors— Ray Bradbury is your man!

"I have not so much thought my way through life as done things and found what it was and who I was after the doing," Ray has said.

What outrageous chances Bradbury has taken in the hundreds of stories he's written since his first major ones in 1945. Only rarely does he fail to convince his readers that this or that amazing tale didn't really happen. Here's a typical and wonderful Bradbury whopper.

In his short story, "The Parrot Who Met Papa," Bradbury involves real names of writers in a marvelous farce. The premise is that, eight years after the death of Ernest Hemingway, El Cordoba, a parrot who lived behind the bar of the author's favorite Havana bar, is kidnapped. The fascinating thing is that the parrot is like a living recorder—plus.

> All during the time Papa had lived in Finca Vigia, he had known the parrot and had talked to him and the parrot had talked back. As the years passed, people said that Hemingway began to talk like the parrot and others said no, the parrot learned to talk like *him*! Papa used to line the drinks up on the counter and sit near the cage and involve that bird in the best kind of conversation you ever heard, four nights running. By the end of the second year, that parrot knew more about Hem and Thomas Wolfe and Sherwood Anderson than Gertrude Stein did. In fact, the parrot even knew who Gertrude Stein *was*. All you had to say was "Gertrude" and the parrot said:
> "Pigeons on the grass, alas."

The narrator suspects the kidnapper to be Shelley Capon (a hysterically droll caricature of that trollish writer Truman Capote, who always hated Hemingway). He finds Capon and the bird in a Havana hotel suite, and he decides to test the parrot, who replies in Hemingway's voice.

> Shelley Capon read my mind. "The effect is better," he said, "with the shawl over the cage."
> I put the shawl back over the bars.
> I was thinking very fast. Then I thought very slowly. I bent and whispered by the cage:
> "Norman Mailer."
> "Couldn't remember the alphabet," said the voice beneath the shawl.
> "Gertrude Stein," I said.
> "Suffered from undescended testicles," said the voice.
> "My God," I gasped.
> I stepped back. I stared at the covered cage. I blinked at Shelley Capon.
> "Do you really *know* what you have here, Capon?"
> "A *gold* mine, dear Raimundo!" he crowed.

"A *mint!*" I corrected.

"Endless opportunities for blackmail!"

"Causes for murder!" I added.

"Think!" Shelley snorted into his drink. "Think what Mailer's publishers *alone* would pay to shut this bird up!"

I spoke to the cage:

"F. Scott Fitzgerald."

Silence.

"Try 'Scottie,'" said Shelley.

"Ah," said the voice inside the cage. "Good left jab but couldn't follow through. Nice contender, but—"

"Faulkner," I said.

"Batting average fair, strictly a singles hitter."

"Steinbeck!"

"Finished last at end of season."

"Ezra Pound!"

"Traded off to the minor leagues in 1932."

"I think...I need...one of those drinks." Someone put a drink in my hand. I gulped it and nodded. I shut my eyes and felt the world give one turn, then opened my eyes to look at Shelley Capon, the classic son of a bitch of all time.

"There is something even more fantastic," he said. "You've heard only the first half."

Capon reveals that even though Hemingway had difficulty writing during his last years, he *told* a whole novel to the parrot who knows it by heart and, if encouraged, repeats it in its entirety! This is potentially the most valuable bird that ever lived, and Capon is determined to exploit it, already receiving lucrative offers from publishers for "Hemingway's last novel." The narrator, determined to thwart Capon's rapacious greed, makes off with the bird and heads for the airport.

The trickiest business—and my greatest danger—remained. I knew that by the time I got to the airport, the guards and the Castro militia would have been alerted. I wouldn't put it past Shelley Capon to tell them that a national treasure was getting away. He might even cut Castro in on some of the Book-of-the-Month Club revenue and the movie rights. I had to im-provise a plan to get through customs.

I am a literary man, however, and the answer came to me quickly. I had the taxi stop long enough for me to buy some shoe polish. I began to apply the disguise to El Córdoba. I painted him black all over.

"Listen," I said bending down to whisper into the cage as we drove across Havana. "*Nevermore.*"

I repeated it several times to give him the idea. The sound would be new to him, because, I guessed, Papa would never have quoted a middleweight contender he had knocked out years ago. There was silence under the shawl while the word was recorded.

Then, at last, it came back to me. "Nevermore," in Papa's old, familiar, tenor voice, "nevermore," it said.

The End

I recently asked Ray Bradbury if "Nevermore" meant the parrot would nevermore quote Hemingway, and he replied:

"Not at all—it was just to complete the bird's raven disguise. Good old Edgar Allan Poe! He is going to talk like Ernest happily ever after!"

ॐ ❖ ॐ

THERE ARE TWO GREAT SCENES IN THE MEMORABLE 1970 FILM *Five Easy Pieces*.

One is heart-breaking:

Bob Dupea (Jack Nicholson), a pianist of promise who has given up his career to work on an oil rig, visits his father after a long separation and tearfully pours out his soul to him. The old man has had a stroke, says nothing in reply, and one doesn't know if he has understood a word.

The other scene, the famous "chicken-salad scene," is side-splitting in the way Nicholson, as the testy Dupea, and Lorna Thayer, as the dead-pan waitress, play it. Written by Adrien Joyce and directed by Bob Rafelson, it goes like this:

Dupea: "I'd like a plain omelet, no potatoes, tomatoes instead. A cup of coffee and toast."

Waitress, pointing to his menu: "No substitutions."

Desperately Nicholson tries to get around the "No substitutions" policy and come up with a way to get a side order of wheat toast.

"I don't make the rules," the waitress, increasingly annoyed, says.

Dupea: "OK, I'll make it as easy for you as I can. I'd like an omelet, plain. And a chicken salad sandwich on wheat toast. No mayonnaise, no butter, no lettuce. And a cup of coffee."

Waitress: "A No. 2, chicken sal sand. Hold the butter, the lettuce and the mayonnaise. And a cup of coffee. Anything else?"

Dupea: "Yeah, now all you have to do is hold the chicken, bring me the toast, give me a check for the chicken salad sandwich, and you haven't broken any rules."

Waitress: "You want me to hold the chicken, huh?"

Dupea: "I want you to hold it between your knees."

Waitress, pointing to the right-to-serve sign. "Do you see that sign, sir? I guess you'll all have to leave. I'm not taking any more of your smartness and sarcasm."

Dupea, having calmly put on his sunglasses and picked up his gloves: "Do you see this sign?"

In a sudden burst, he sweeps his arm across the table, sending the water glasses, silverware and menus flying.

The scene, which is considered quintessential Nicholson, has had a long afterlife—and it is frequently quoted and misquoted around Hollywood watering holes.

❧ ❖ ☙

ONE ASSOCIATES GRAHAM GREENE'S NAME WITH SOPHISTICATED thrillers, like *The Third Man*. But he could also write quiet, bittersweet humor, such as his 1967 story "A Shocking Accident" from his book *May We Borrow Your Husband?*

Here is how the story begins.

Jerome was called into his housemaster's room in the break between the second and the third class on a Thursday morning. He had no fear of trouble, for he was a warden—the name that the proprietor and headmaster of a rather expensive preparatory school had chosen to give to approved reliable boys in the lower forms (from a warden one became a guardian and finally before leaving, it was hoped for Marlborough or Rugby, a crusader). The housemaster, Mr. Wordsworth, sat behind his desk with an appearance of perplexity and apprehension. Jerome had the odd impression when he entered that he was a cause of fear.

"Sit down, Jerome," Mr. Wordsworth said. "All going well with the trigonometry?"

"Yes, sir."

"I've had a telephone call, Jerome. From your aunt. I'm afraid I have bad news for you."

"Yes, sir?"

"Your father has had an accident."

"Oh."

Mr. Wordsworth looked at him with some surprise. "A serious accident."

"Yes, sir?"

Jerome worshipped his father: the verb is exact. As man re-creates God, so Jerome re-created his father—from a restless widowed author into a mysterious adventurer who traveled in far places—Nice, Beirut, Majorca, even the Canaries. The time had arrived about his eighth birthday when Jerome believed that his father either "ran guns" or was a member of the British Secret Service. Now it occurred to him that his father might have been wounded in "a hail of machine-gun bullets."

Mr. Wordsworth played with the ruler on his desk. He seemed at a loss how to continue. He said, "You knew your father was in Naples?"

"Yes, sir."

"Your aunt heard from the hospital today."

"Oh."

Mr. Wordsworth said with desperation: "It was a street accident."

"Yes, sir?" It seemed quite likely to Jerome that they would call it a street accident. The police, of course, had fired first; his father would not take human life except as a last resort.

"I'm afraid your father was very seriously hurt indeed."

"Oh."

"In fact, Jerome, he died yesterday. Quite without pain."

"Did they shoot him through the heart?"

"I beg your pardon. What did you say, Jerome?"

"Did they shoot him through the heart?"

"Nobody shot him, Jerome. A pig fell on him." An inexplicable convulsion took place in the nerves of Mr. Wordsworth's face; it really looked for a moment as though he were going to laugh. He closed his eyes, composed his features, and said rapidly, as though it were necessary to expel the story as rapidly as possible. "Your father was walking along a street in Naples when a pig fell on him. A shocking accident. Apparently in the poorer quarters of Naples they keep pigs on their balconies. This one was on the fifth floor. It had grown too fat. The balcony broke. The pig fell on your father."

Mr. Wordsworth left his desk rapidly and went to the window, turning his back on Jerome. He shook a little with emotion

Jerome said, "What happened to the pig?"

Jerome is not being callous—he is only trying to visualize the strange scene and get the details right.

The pig story haunts Jerome and follows him into adulthood. Amazingly enough, this tale which starts out almost farcically becomes totally believable and poignant as it goes along. Such is the magic of a great writer!

At the end of the story, Jerome has met and fallen in love with the girl of his dreams. But dare he tell her the story of his father's bizarre death which everyone he's ever told has laughed at? He finally gets up nerve enough to tell her. She says, "How horrible" and then adds, "I was wondering, what happened to the poor pig?" And Jerome knows he has met his mate for life.

૭ ❖ ౮

THERE ARE SO MANY KINDS OF HUMOR, SO MANY DIFFERENT WAYS OF eliciting a chuckle, a grin, or maybe just a wry shake of the head. Here is a noir scene from a book all of America was reading and shaking their heads over half a century ago.

> ❝ There are so many kinds of humor, so many different ways of eliciting a chuckle, a grin, or maybe just a wry shake of the head. ❞

The book was Evelyn Waugh's outrageous novel *The Loved One*. This is the story of a young and poetic Englishman, Dennis Barlow, who works in a pet cemetery in Los Angeles, called The Happier Hunting Ground. He falls in love with a lovely dimwit, Aimée Thanatogenos, who works as a "cosmetician" for the departed loved ones at nearby Whispering Glades, a dead—(in every sense of the word)—ringer for Forest Lawn.

The revered English poet, Alfred Noyes, he who wrote "The Highwayman" that everyone learned in high school in those days, handed me the book in 1948. (I couldn't believe this classic writer of classics was still alive, but I was very young and he was very old.)

"Must read it, old chap," the ancient author said chuckling. "Absolutely appalling!"

At Dennis' place of work, pet cats, parrots, goats, whatever, get a proper burial, even including a religious service if requested, and each year a commemorative card is sent to the bereaved owner, saying "Your little (pet's name) is in Heaven, thinking of you." In the case of dogs it was "Your little (pet's name) is wagging his tail in Heaven tonight, thinking of you."

Aimée loves Dennis, but she doesn't know he works for a mere pet funeral home; she loves her profession and wants to rise in the *proper* type of funeral business. The fatuous Senior Mortician at Whispering Glades, Mr. Joyboy, is crazy about Aimée and wants to marry her. But so does Dennis. She is in a total state of confusion, especially when she discovers that Dennis works for a lowly pet cemetery and didn't write—as she had thought—the poems he's always quoting.

After consulting her Guru, she decides the only way out is to cease being a "Waiting One" and become "A Loved One," which was most easily accomplished by suicide; this plan she executes in Mr. Joyboy's office.

Horrified at the possible scandal to Whispering Glades, the mortician enlists Dennis' aid to get rid of Aimée's body.

Mr. Joyboy was waiting for Dennis at the side entrance

of the mortuary. Whispering Glades was ideally equipped for the smooth movement of bodies. On a swift and silent trolley they set Dennis's largest collecting-box, first empty, later full. They drove to the Happier Hunting Ground where things were more makeshift but between them without great difficulty they man-handled their load to the crematorium, and stowed it in the oven. Dennis turned on the gas and lit it. Flame shot from all sides of the brick oven. He closed the iron door.

"I reckon she'll take an hour and a half," he said. "Do you want to stay?"

"I can't bear to think of her going out like this—she loved to see things done right."

"I rather thought of conducting a service. My first and last non-sectarian office."

"I couldn't bear that," said Mr. Joyboy.

"Very well. I will recite instead a little poem I have written for the occasion.

"Aimée, thy beauty was to me,
Like those Nicean barks of yore,"

"Hey, you can't say that. That's the phony poem."
"Joyboy, please remember where you are."

"That gently, o'er a perfumed sea
The weary way-worn wanderer bore
To his own native shore."

"It's really remarkably apposite, is it not?"
But Mr. Joyboy had left the building.

The fire roared in the brick oven. Dennis must wait until all was consumed. Meanwhile he entered the office and made a note in the book kept there for that purpose.

Tomorrow, and on every anniversary as long as the Happier Hunting Ground existed, a postcard would go to Mr. Joyboy: *Your little Aimée is wagging her tail in heaven tonight, thinking of you.*

For some time everyone in America and England was quoting that last line to each other.

In the 1965 film Dennis was played by Robert Morse, Mr. Joyboy by Rod Steiger. Also in the cast were Anjanette Comer, Jonathan Winters, Liberace, Milton Berle, and John Gielgud. It was correctly advertised as "the picture with something to offend everyone."

ಎ ❖ ಣ

IT IS A DIFFICULT DECISION WHETHER TO PLACE EVELYN WAUGH'S masterful, satiric, delightful, and chilling 1934 novel, *A Handful of Dust*, in the *Horror* or the *Humor* category. One laughs, one cries, just like the Greek masks. It is perhaps more bizarre than humorous, but a great writer can make the most bizarre of scenes become not only inevitable but totally believable; Waugh has that genius.

In *A Handful of Dust*, Tony Last goes through a hurtful but commonplace divorce in London's fashionable society. To get away he goes on an expedition to South America. Somehow, in the upper Amazon, Tony is stranded in a remote village in the hut of a fellow Englishman, the eccentric Mr. Todd. Tony is appreciative of the fact that he has been helped by Mr. Todd and is pleased to reward him, while waiting to be rescued, by indulging him by reading from his beloved Dickens' collection. When a rescue group comes near looking for him, Mr. Todd drugs Tony.

> Tony gulped the dark liquid, trying not to taste it. But it was not unpleasant, hard and muddy on the palate like most of the beverages he had been offered in Brazil, but with a flavor of honey and brown bread. He leant back in the hammock feeling unusually contented. Perhaps at that very moment the search party was in camp a few hours journey from them. Meanwhile he was warm and drowsy. The cadence of song rose and fell interminably, liturgically. Another calabash of *piwari* was offered him and he handed it back empty. He lay full length, watching the play of shadows on the thatch as the Pie-wies began to dance. Then he shut his eyes and thought of England and Hetton and fell asleep.
>
> He awoke, still in the Indian hut, with the impression that he had outslept his usual hour. By the position of the sun

he knew it was late afternoon. No one else was about. He looked for his watch and found to his surprise that it was not on his wrist. He had left it in the house, he supposed, before coming to the party.

"I must have been tight last night," he reflected. "Treacherous drink that." He had a headache and feared a recurrence of fever. He found when he set his feet to the ground that he stood with difficulty; his walk was unsteady and his mind confused as it had been during the first weeks of his convalescence. On the way across the savannah he was obliged to stop more than once, shutting his eyes and breathing deeply. When he reached the house he found Mr. Todd sitting there.

"Ah, my friend, you are late for the reading this afternoon. There is scarcely another half hour of light. How do you feel?"

"Rotten. That drink doesn't seem to agree with me."

"I will give you something to make you better. The forest has remedies for everything: to make you awake and to make you sleep."

"You haven't seen my watch anywhere?"

"You have missed it?"

"Yes. I thought I was wearing it. I say, I've never slept so long."

"Not since you were a baby. Do you know how long? Two days."

"Nonsense. I can't have."

"Yes, indeed. It is a long time. It is a pity because you missed our guests."

"Guests?"

"Why, yes. I have been quite gay while you were asleep. Three men from outside. Englishmen. It is a pity you missed them. A pity for them, too, as they particularly wished to see you. But what could I do? You were so sound asleep. They had come all the way to find you, so—I thought you would not mind—as you could not greet them yourself I gave them a little souvenir, your watch. They wanted something to take back to England where a reward is being offered for news of you. They were very pleased with it. And they took some photographs of the little cross I put up to commemorate your coming. They were pleased with that, too. They were very easily pleased. But I do not suppose they will visit us again, our life here is so retired,...no pleasures except reading...I do not suppose we shall ever have visitors again...well, well, I will get you some medicine to make you feel better. Your head aches, does it not?...We will not have any Dickens today...but tomorrow, and the day after that, and the day after that. Let us read *Little Dorrit* again. There are passages in that book I can never hear without the temptation to weep."

Poor Tony—he is sentenced to a Dickensian life in the jungle.

ဆာ ❖ ઄

WITH ABOUT HALF A DOZEN VICIOUS MURDERS OCCURRING throughout the play, *Macbeth* can hardly be called a bowl of laughs, but no one understood the value of comic relief better than William Shakespeare—hence the brief scene in Act II, scene three, where a drunken porter holds forth on the joys and pitfalls of the consumption of what W. C. Fields was to refer to as "Spiritus Fermentae."

Inverness. MACBETH'S castle

Knocking within. Enter a PORTER.

PORTER. Here's a knocking indeed! If a man were porter of hell-gate, he should have old turning the key. [*Knock*] Knock, knock, knock! Who's there, I' th' name of Beelzebub? Here's a farmer that hang'd himself on th' expectation of plenty. Come in time; have napkins enow about you; here you'll sweat for't. [*Knock*] Knock, knock! Who's there, i' th' other devil's name? Faith, here's an equivocator, that could swear in both the scales against either scale; who committed treason enough for God's sake, yet could not equivocate to heaven. O, come in, equivocator. [*Knock*] Knock, knock, knock! Who's there? Faith, here's an English tailor come hither for stealing out of a French hose. Come in, tailor, here you may roast your goose. [*Knock*] Knock, knock; never at quiet! What are you? But this place is too cold for hell. I'll devil-porter it no further. I had thought to have let in some of all professions that go the primrose way to th' everlasting bonfire. [*Knock*] Anon, anon! [*Opens the gate*] I pray you remember the porter.

Enter MACDUFF and LENNOX

MACDUFF. Was it so late, friend, ere you went to bed, that you do lie so late?

PORTER. Faith, sir, we were carousing till the second cock; and drink, sir, is a great provoker of three things.

MACDUFF. What three things does drink especially provoke?

PORTER. Marry, sir, nose-painting, sleep, and urine. Lechery, sir, it provokes and unprovokes: it provokes the desire, but it takes away the performance. Therefore much drink may be said to be an equivocator with lechery: it makes him, and it mars him; it sets him on, and it takes him off; it persuades him, and disheartens him; makes him stand to, and not stand to in conclusion, equivocates him in a sleep, and, giving him the lie, leaves him.

MACDUFF. I believe drink gave thee the lie last night.

PORTER. That it did, sir, i' the very throat on me; but I requited him for his lie; and, I think, being too strong for him, though he took up my legs sometime, yet I made a shift to cast him.

MACDUFF. Is thy master stirring?

Enter MACBETH

Our knocking has awak'd him; here he comes.

There is a great many humorous scenes in Shakespeare, some of them ribald, all of them appropriate, all of them superbly written and worthy of study.

ဢ ❖ ಪ

THE GREAT STORY-TELLER ELMORE LEONARD HAS WARNED WRITERS: "Tell a dream—lose a reader."

The dream-gimmick has been a beloved one of beginning writers for a long, long time—"and then just as the tiger was about to get me, I woke up!" It is usually very unsatisfactory, although it certainly worked for Lewis Carroll whose Alice wakes up at the end from her Wonderland dream just after the Queen has bellowed "off with her head!"

Another writer, Thomas Meehan, got away with it splendidly in his fey *New Yorker* magazine story "Yma Dream." It begins:

> In this dream, which I have had on the night of the full moon for the past three months, I am giving a cocktail party in honor of Yma Sumac, the Peruvian singer. This is strange at once, for while I have unbounded admiration for four-octave voices, I have never met Miss Sumac, and, even in a dream, it seems unlikely that I should be giving her a party. No matter. She and I are in the small living room of my apartment, on Charles Street, in Greenwich Village, and we are getting along famously. I have told her several of my Swedish-dialect stories, and she had reciprocated by singing for me, in Quechua, a medley of Andean folk songs. Other guests are expected momentarily. I have no idea, however, who any of them will be.
>
> The first guest who comes in is Ava Gardner.
>
> "Ava, Yma," I say.
>
> The next guest is Abba Eban, former Israeli Ambassador to the United Nations, and then Oona O'Neill.
>
> "Oona, Yma; Oona, Ava; Oona, Abba," I say.

The ludicrous introductions go on with the arrivals of novelist Ira Wolfert, Ilya Ehrenburg, the Russian novelist, Ugo Belti, the Italian playwright and the actress Ona Munson and

Ida Lupino—plus the Aga Kahn. Actresses Eva Gabor and then Uta Hagen come in to complete the group.

> "Please have the common decency to introduce your guests to one another," says Miss Sumac, in a cold monotone. "And in the proper manner."
>
> In the dream, Yma Sumac seems to have some kind of hold over me, and I must do as she wishes. "O.K., O.K.," I snap crossly. "Uta, Yma; Uta, Ava; Uta, Oona; Uta, Ona; Uta, Ida; Uta, Ugo; Uta, Abba; Uta, Ilya; Uta, Ira; Uta, Aga; Uta, Eva."

The story, which is beginning to sound like feeding time in the chimpanzee compound, ends like this:

> In the hope that no further company will arrive, I silently close the door. The bell rings instantly, however, and I feel a chill run down my spine. I pretend not to hear it.
>
> "Answer the door," Miss Sumac says peremptorily. My circle of guests moves menacingly toward me. With a plummeting heart, I open the door. Standing before me, in immaculate evening dress, is a sturdy, distinguished-looking man. He is the Polish concert pianist Mieczyslaw Horszowski.
>
> "Come in, Mieczyslaw!" I cry, with tears in my eyes. "I've never been so glad to see anyone in my whole life!"
>
> And here always, my dream ends.

I think author Meehan missed the chance for a fine final snapper; his joy at seeing the Polish pianist should disappear when he realizes that the young woman on his arm is the actress, Miss Thurman—and it's back to work.

(Thomas Meehan wrote the Tony-winning book for the musical *Annie* and collaborated with Mel Brooks on the stage version of *The Producers*.)

☙ ❖ ❧

ONE OF AMERICA'S MOST CONSISTENTLY FUNNY COLUMNISTS IS Dave Barry, whose column was syndicated all over the country. His stockin-trade is total nonsense, but even so he is always thinking in terms of scenes, such as this "historical" account.

> A traditional thing you should do is teach your kids the true meaning of Thanksgiving. I suggest you have them put on the following historical play, "The Very First Thanksgiving," which I wrote myself after several back-breaking minutes of research in the encyclopedia.

THE VERY FIRST THANKSGIVING

> *SCENE ONE: Some Pilgrims are standing on the deck of the Mayflower.*

FIRST PILGRIM: Well, here it is, the year 1620.

SECOND PILGRIM: Yes, and we have been on this tiny ship, the Mayflower, for many weeks, fleeing persecution in England because of our religious views.

FOURTH PILGRIM: Also, we wear hats that look like traffic cones.

FIRST PILGRIM: What happened to the Third Pilgrim?

SECOND PILGRIM: He's throwing up.

FOURTH PILGRIM: Hey, look! There's Plymouth Rock! Pull over, captain!

LONG JOHN SILVER: Arrr, Matey.

> *SCENE TWO: The Pilgrims are standing on the shore.*

FIRST PILGRIM: Well, this looks like a barren area with poor soil and harsh winters, offering little chance for our survival.

OTHER PILGRIMS: Perfect!

SECOND PILGRIM: Look! A Native American!

NATIVE AMERICAN: Fortunately, I speak English. My name is Squanto.

FOURTH PILGRIM: "Squanto"? What kind of name is "Squanto"?

SECOND PILGRIM: It sounds nasty! It sounds like, "Mom! The dog made Squanto on the linoleum!"

FIRST PILGRIM: What's "linoleum"?

SECOND PILGRIM: I have no idea.

SCENE THREE: One year later.

FIRST PILGRIM: Well, here it is, one year later.

SECOND PILGRIM: That was a pretty harsh winter.

FOURTH PILGRIM: That was definitely the last winter I plan to spend in a small confined space with people eating a diet of maize and beans.

FIRST PILGRIM: Also, as you will recall, we had a lot of starvation and disease, the result being that half of us are dead.

SECOND PILGRIM: Time for a celebration!

SCENE FOUR: The Pilgrims and Squanto are seated at a banquet table.

FIRST PILGRIM: So here we are, at the (burp) first Thanksgiving.

SECOND PILGRIM: I definitely want the recipe for this ale-wife dip.

FOURTH PILGRIM: Hey Squanto, what are those drums saying?

SQUANTO (after listening for a moment): They say "Lions 14, Bears 7."

FIRST PILGRIM: You know, Squanto, without your help, we never would have survived this winter. So we've decided to take over all of North America and pretty much obliterate your culture.

SQUANTO: Sure.

FIRST PILGRIM: Really? You don't mind?

SQUANTO: No, not at all.

FIRST PILGRIM: Great!

SQUANTO: Try this stuffing.

In this piece, as you can see, Barry deftly uses a script format and understated dialogue as well as a fatuous approach to the subject matter to create the humor.

℘ ❖ ℘

THE FOLLOWING LONG SCENE IS NOT EXACTLY HAH-HAH COMEDY—actually, it is from a superb story of character, but I guarantee that you will smile at the end, so we will term it a semi-comedy here.

This is from a master of the short story, W. Somerset Maugham, and it is called "Mr. Know-All."

The narrator is on a Japan-bound liner and his cabin-mate happens to be an obnoxious gentleman, Max Kelada, whom he instantly dislikes.

Shortly after their meeting, pushy Max comes over to the table where the narrator is playing patience.

"The three on the four," said Mr. Kelada.

There is nothing more exasperating when you are playing patience than to be told where to put the card you have turned up before you have had a chance to look for yourself.

"It's coming out, it's coming out," he cried. "The ten on the knave."

With rage and hatred in my heart I finished. Then he seized the pack.

"Do you like card tricks?"

"No, I hate card tricks," I answered.

"Well, I'll just show you this one."

He showed me three. Then I said I would go down to the dining-room and get my seat at table.

"Oh, that's all right," he said. "I've already taken a seat for you. I thought that as we were in the same state-room we might just as well sit at the same table."

I did not like Mr. Kelada.

On board they meet Ramsay, a young American consular officer and his beautiful, shy wife who have been reunited after a year's separation because of his duties. At dinner the conversation gets around to pearls.

As on all subjects, Mr. Know-All, as they have dubbed him, is an expert on pearls.

"Well, I ought to know what I am talking about, I'm going to Japan just to look into this Japanese pearl business. I'm in the trade and there's not a man in it who won't tell you that what I say about pearls goes. I know all the best pearls in the world, and what I don't know about pearls isn't worth knowing."

Here was news for us, for Mr. Kelada, with all his loquacity, had never told anyone what his business was. We only knew vaguely that he was going to Japan on some commercial errand. He looked round the table triumphantly.

"They'll never be able to get a cultured pearl that an expert like me can't tell with half an eye." He pointed to a chain that Mrs. Ramsay wore. "You take my word for it, Mrs. Ramsay, that chain you're wearing will never be worth a cent less than it is now."

Mrs. Ramsay in her modest way flushed a little and slipped the chain inside her dress. Ramsay leaned forward. He gave us all a look and a smile flickered in his eyes.

"That's a pretty chain of Mrs. Ramsay's, isn't it?"

"I noticed it at once," answered Mr. Kelada. "Gee, I said to myself, those are pearls all right."

"I didn't buy it myself, of course. I'd be interested to know how much you think it cost."

"Oh, in the trade somewhere round fifteen thousand dollars. But if it was bought on Fifth Avenue I shouldn't be surprised to hear that anything up to thirty thousand was paid for it."

Ramsay smiled grimly.

"You'll be surprised to hear that Mrs. Ramsay bought that string at a department store the day before we left New York, for eighteen dollars."

Mr. Kelada flushed.

"Rot. It's not only real, but it's as fine a string for its size as I've ever seen."

"Will you bet on it? I'll bet you a hundred dollars it's imitation."

"Done."

"Oh, Elmer, you can't bet on a certainty," said Mrs. Ramsay.

She had a little smile on her lips and her tone was gently deprecating.

"Can't I? If I get a chance of easy money like that I should be all sorts of a fool not to take it."

"But how can it be proved?" she continued. "It's only my word against Mr. Kelada's."

"Let me look at the chain, and if it's imitation I'll tell you quickly enough. I can afford to lose a hundred dollars," said Mr. Kelada.

"Take it off, dear. Let the gentleman look at it as much as he wants."

Mrs. Ramsay hesitated a moment. She put her hands to the clasp.

"I can't undo it," she said. "Mr. Kelada will just have to take my word for it."

I had a sudden suspicion that something unfortunate was about to occur, but I could think of nothing to say.

Ramsay jumped up.

"I'll undo it."

He handed the chain to Mr. Kelada. The Levantine took a magnifying glass from his pocket and closely examined it. A smile of triumph spread over his smooth and swarthy face. He handed back the chain. He was about to speak. Suddenly he caught sight of Mrs. Ramsay's face. It was so white that she looked as though she were about to faint. She was staring at him with wide and terrified eyes. They held a desperate appeal; it was so clear that I wondered why her husband did not see it.

Mr. Kelada stopped with his mouth open. He flushed deeply. You could almost see the effort he was making over himself.

"I was mistaken," he said. "It's a very good imitation, but of course as soon as I looked through my glass I saw that it wasn't real. I think eighteen dollars is just about as much as the damned thing's worth."

He took out his pocket-book and from it a hundred-dollar note. He handed it to Ramsay without a word.

"Perhaps that'll teach you not to be so cocksure another time, my young friend," said Ramsay as he took the note.

I noticed that Mr. Kelada's hands were trembling.

The story spread over the ship as stories do, and he had to put up with a good deal of chaff that evening. It was a fine joke that Mr. Know-All had been caught out. But Mrs. Ramsay retired to her state-room with a headache.

Next morning I got up and began to shave. Mr. Kelada lay on his bed smoking a cigarette. Suddenly there was a small scraping sound and I saw a letter pushed under the door. I opened the door and looked out. There was nobody there. I picked up the letter and saw that it was addressed. to Max Kelada. The name was written in block letters. I handed it to him.

"Who's this from?" He opened it. "Oh!"

He took out of the envelope, not a letter, but a hundred-dollar note. He looked at me and again he reddened. He tore the envelope into little bits and gave them to me.

"Do you mind just throwing them out of the port-hole?"

I did as he asked, and then I looked at him with a smile.

"No one likes being made to look a perfect damned fool," he said.

"Were the pearls real?"

"If I had a pretty little wife, I shouldn't let her spend a year in New York while I stayed at Kobe," said he.

At that moment I did not entirely dislike Mr. Kelada. He reached out for his pocket-book and carefully put in it the hundred-dollar note.

In one brilliant scene at the end of this story we see conflict involving a well-drawn character who we thought we disliked thoroughly, we have the narrator change his opinion of the man, we the readers change our opinion of the man, and we learn of a great choice made.

In other words, you have here a perfect example of the essentials of a good story—the Five C's:

Characters, Conflict, Choice, Change, and Compassion

(And as for the "s" of the five "C"'s, I volunteer "*surprise*", which also shows up in this story.)

Curiously, the great French writer, Guy De Maupassant, has a story somewhat similar: a young, beautiful, loving, and apparently faithful wife has a passion for what she tells her adoring husband is junk jewelry. She dies unexpectedly, and to his dismay he discovers that her "costume" jewelry is actually worth a fortune, acquired, obviously, by the same ancient technology as Mrs. Ramsay's.

The story is called "The Jewelry." A similar plot is in the Henry James story, "Paste."

Proving, once again, the old adage: "If it's good, it probably isn't new—and if it's new, it probably isn't good."

ഌ ❖ ඌ

THE BRILLIANT HUMORIST CHRISTOPHER BUCKLEY WRITES SHORT pieces for the *New Yorker* and best-selling novels like *No Way To Treat a First Lady*, the prologue of which starts with this attention grabbing first paragraph:

> Babette Van Anka had made love to the President of the United States on eleven previous occasions, but she still couldn't resist inserting "Mr. President" into "Oh, baby, baby, baby." He had told her on the previous occasions that he did not like being called this while, as he put it, congress was in session.

Buckley then gives us a steamy two-page description of the version of "Congress in session" which takes place in the Lincoln Bedroom down the hall from where the First Lady is sleeping. Then this scene:

> Elizabeth Tyler McMann, First Lady of the United States, lay awake in her own still-crisp sheets, looking out the window toward the Washington Monument. Being married to America's most prominent symbol of virility, she was not blind to the irony of finding herself in bed alone, staring at the nation's most prominent phallic symbol. Not much had ever been lost on Beth McMann, other than happiness.
>
> Following the dinner for the President of Uruguay, Beth and the President had left their remaining guests and gone upstairs at 11:30. They'd undressed and gotten into bed. She'd fallen asleep. She had woken up, at 1:42 a.m. by the digital bedside clock, thirsty for water, to find herself alone. Sometimes when a call came in the middle of the night, he went into his study so as not to disturb her. If it was a crisis of some sort, he usually went downstairs to the Oval Office. If it was really pressing, he would go to the Situation Room in the basement of the West Wing so that the press secretary could inform the press that the President had monitored the situation from the Situation Room. This sounded more impressive than "on the phone in bed."

The dark thought crossed Beth's mind, though she really—really—preferred not to consider the possibility, that her husband was down the hall in the Lincoln Bedroom. Surely he wouldn't pull something like that. Surely.

She knew the rumors and, moreover, knew the truth about her philandering husband of many years. But even if the rumors were true, this was the one night it was safe to assume that her husband and Babette Van Anka, actress, singer, party fund raiser, were not engaging in bilateral relations.

Beth sat up in bed, straining to convince herself that her husband was at this very minute downstairs issuing orders to attack some Middle Eastern, or possibly Asian, bounty with stealth weaponry.

Just then she heard the click of the opening door as her husband, the President of the United States, came in.

She knew. Knew instantly, even in the dark. No surer radar than a wife's intuition has been invented.

Beth contemplated doing nothing, waiting until morning, when after freshly squeezed orange juice, toast with butter and marmalade, and black coffee, she could calmly confront him with this latest installment in his serial infidelity. Then pour the coffeepot on his offending parts. She contemplated this for five seconds, then flicked on the light.

He reacted like any creature of the night—raccoon, cockroach—suddenly bathed in unwelcome illumination. There was rapid, lateral darting of the eyes, assessing avenues of flight. He was bent forward oddly, holding his jacket over his groin. Beth interpreted this posture as defensive. The body language shouted, "I've been screwing our guest."

"Iraq," he said with a sigh. He rolled his eyes to show how grave and yet predictable was the situation. It occurred to Beth that Iraq now stood in danger. He might well wait until she had gone back to sleep, then slink off to the Situation Room and order a few cruise missiles launced at Baghdad so that by breakfast time he could look her straight in the eyes.

The argument that followed was boisterous even by the standards of the MacMann marriage, currently in its twenty-fifth and final year.

Early the next day:

Sophie Williams, the White House maid who always brought the First Lady her breakfast, knocked softly and entered. She and Beth exchanged the usual pleasantries as she placed the breakfast tray, with freshly cut orchid, over Beth's lap.

It was at this point that Sophie said to the First Lady softly but with alarm that the President's eyes and mouth were "wide open" and that was "looking awfully still."

He is, indeed, dead as a doornail—and not long after these scenes the First Lady will be charged with murder in the first degree. Is she guilty? did she brain him? Well, the reader is compelled to continue turning the pages to find out—and even when writing humor—

That is the name of the game!

ℰ ❖ ℛ

OF ALL THE MANY FUNNY SCENES IN *THE PINK PANTHER* SERIES, written by Blake Edwards (based on the French *A Shot in the Dark*) which began in 1964, starring Peter Sellers as the bumbling Inspector Clouseau, and directed by Blake Edwards, perhaps the one that is most quickly remembered and quoted is the exchange between Clouseau and a hotel clerk:

> Pointing to dog: "Does your diggy bite?"
> "No."
> Dog bites Clouseau.
> Indignantly: "You said your diggy didn't bite!"
> Clerk: "That's not my diggy."

ℰ ❖ ℛ

SOMETIMES, BUT VERY RARELY, A CARTOON STRIP CAN PRODUCE A scene—an actual scene—which stays in the memory forever. Of all the cartoonists, Charles Schulz created that kind of scene most frequently.

He told me that the one that he received the most mail about in fifty years of producing the cartoon strip "Peanuts" was this one and, as Schulz quipped, "And Snoopy wasn't even in it!"

Charlie Brown, Linus, and Lucy are lying on a little hill looking up at the sky. Lucy says, "Aren't the clouds beautiful? They look like big balls of cotton..."

In the next panel she says, "I could just lie here all day, and watch them drift by..."

In the following panel she adds, "If you use your imagination, you can see lots of things in the cloud formations...What do you think you see, Linus?"

And he says, "Well, those clouds up there look to me like the map of the British Honduras on the Caribbean...that cloud up there looks a little like the profile of Thomas Eakins, the famous painter and sculptor...and that group of clouds over there gives me the impression of the stoning of Stephen...I can see the Apostle Paul standing there to one side..."

And Lucy says, "Uh, huh...that's very good...What do *you* see in the clouds, Charlie Brown?"

And the hapless Charlie says, "Well, I was going to say I saw a ducky and a horsie, but I changed my mind!"

A creative writing class could make good use of this scene to illustrate how economically one can delineate characters with just a few lines of dialogue.

ൟ ❖ ൠ

THE MAN WHO CAME TO DINNER, 1939, WAS ONE OF THE MOST popular comedies to ever hit Broadway though it seems very dated now. It told the story of the famous writer, Sheridan Whiteside, brilliant but irascible and demanding, who is in a small Midwest town on a lecture tour when he breaks his leg at the home of the nice normal Stanley family. He is forced to spend weeks there recovering, during which time he meddles in their lives and drives everyone slightly crazy. The audience finally sees the Great Man in Scene One, but only after they hear him bellowing from his room at his doctor—"You're a quack if I ever saw one!"—and at his nurse, Miss Bedpan as he calls her—"Great dribbling cow!" Finally the moment of his appearance approaches and there is great anticipation.

MRS. STANLEY (*all eagerness*): You mean he's coming out now?

JOHN appears in doorway up R.C.

MAGGIE (*moves chair up* C. *of desk*). (*Quietly.*): He is indeed.

MRS. MCCUTCHEON (*rises, crosses* D.L.): He's coming out!

MRS. DEXTER (*crossing to Mrs. McCutcheon D.L.*): I can hardly wait!

MRS. STANLEY: Ernest, call June. June! June! Mr. Whiteside is coming out!

JOHN (*beckoning to Sarah off U.R.*): Sarah! Sarah! Mr. Whiteside is coming out!

MRS. STANLEY: I'm so excited I just don't know what to do!

MRS. DEXTER: Me too! I know that I'll simply—

On the stairs, MRS. STANLEY and the two other ladies are keenly expectant; even Stanley is on the qui vive. The double doors are opened once more and Dr. Bradley appears, bag in hand, D.R. He has taken a good deal of punishment, and speaks with a rather false heartiness.

MRS. STANLEY: Good morning, Dr. Bradley.

A moment's pause, and then a wheelchair is rolled through the door by the nurse. It is full of pillows, blankets, and Sheridan Whiteside. Sheridan Whiteside is indeed portly and Falstaffian. He is wearing an elaborate velvet smoking-jacket and a very loud tie, and he looks like every caricature ever drawn of him. There is a hush as the wheelchair rolls into the room D.R. Welcoming smiles break over every face. The chair comes to a halt; Whiteside looks slowly around, into each and every beaming face. His fingers drum for a moment on the arm of the chair. He looks slowly around once more. Maggie comes D.R. Dr. Bradley crosses to the wheel-chair, then Mrs. Stanley. She laughs nervously. And then HE speaks.

WHITESIDE *(R.C., quietly to Maggie)*: I may vomit.

MRS. STANLEY *(with a nervous little laugh)*: Good morning, Mr. Whiteside. I'm Mrs. Ernest Stanley—remember. And this is Mr. Stanley.

STANLEY *(coming to D.C.)*: How do you do, Mr. Whiteside? I hope that you are better.

WHITESIDE: Thank you. I am suing you for a hundred and fifty thousand dollars.

STANLEY: How's that? What?

WHITESIDE: I said I am suing you for a hundred and fifty thousand dollars.

The play was written by the great team of George Kaufman and Moss Hart who had so many other hits on Broadway, and was based on the character of the acerbic and effete pundit, Alexandeer Woolcut. The part was played to perfection by Monty Wooley and, *mirabile dictu*, again in the 1941 film with Bette Davis and Jimmy Dsurante.

No star, before or since, has had an opening line so memorable as: "I may vomit."

11

Horror

———

Any writer who treasures the delicious shock of James Whale's 1931 film *Frankenstein*, with the marvelous scene in the creepy laboratory with the creepy hunchbacked assistant, the weird flagons and machinery, and the dramatic lightning strikes as the monster comes to life, might be disappointed in reading the source material.

In the original 1818 book by Mary Shelley, often called the first science fiction novel, the monster is not a mindless, inarticulate creature with bolts in his neck and stitches still in his head. He is graceful, intelligent and can read and write. He *is* eight feet tall and very ugly, but there is no Igor, the creature's brain did not come from a criminal corpse, and there is no howling mob of villagers with torches and no burning mill. Incredibly, the novel begins and ends in "the frozen North" for reasons too complicated to explain.

Apparently the novel was a result of a weekend party in Geneva where Mary Shelley and her poet husband, Percy, vied with Lord Byron to see who could write the spookiest story. Mary won, but it took her a year to expand and finish the novel. It was an instant success and has never been out of print.

The author does not give the reader many details of how Dr. Victor Frankenstein created his monster, or how he found the secret of life.

> It was with these feelings that I began the creation of a human being. As the minuteness of the parts formed a great hindrance to my speed, I resolved, contrary to my first intention, to make the being of a gigantic stature, that is to say, about eight feet in height, and proportionably large. After having

formed this determination and having spent some months in successfully collecting and arranging my materials, I began.

No one can conceive the variety of feelings which bore me onwards, like a hurricane, in the first enthusiasm of success. Life and death appeared to me ideal bounds, which I should first break through, and pour a torrent of light into our dark world. A new species would bless me as its creator and source; many happy and excellent natures would owe their being to me.

At last the big day—or rather, night—arrived:

It was on a dreary night of November that I beheld the accomplishment of my toils. With an anxiety that almost amounted to agony, I collected the instruments of life around me, that I might infuse a spark of being into the lifeless thing that lay at my feet. It was already one in the morning; the rain pattered dismally against the panes, and my candle was nearly burnt out, when, by the glimmer of the half-extinguished light, I saw the dull yellow eye of the creature open; it breathed hard, and a convulsive motion agitated its limbs.

How can I describe my emotions at this catastrophe, or how delineate the wretch whom with such infinite pains and care I had endeavoured to form? His limbs were in proportion, and I had selected his features as beautiful. Beautiful! Great God! His yellow skin scarcely covered the work of muscles and arteries beneath; his hair was of a lustrous black, and flowing; his teeth of a pearly whiteness; but these luxuriances only formed a more horrid contrast with his watery eyes, that seemed almost of the same colour as the dun-white sockets in which they were set, his shriveled complexion and straight black lips.

The different accidents of life are not so changeable as the feelings of human nature. I had worked hard for the nearly two years, for the sole purpose of infusing life into an inanimate body. For this I had deprived myself of rest and health. I had desired it with an ardour that far exceeded moderation; but now that I had finished, the beauty of the dream vanished, and breathless horror and disgust filled my heart. Unable to endure the aspect of the being I had created, I rushed out of the room and continued a long time traversing my bedchamber, unable to compose my mind to sleep. At length lassitude succeeded to the tumult I had before endured, and I threw myself on the bed in my clothes, endeavouring to seek a few moments of forgetfulness. But it was in vain; I slept, indeed, but I was disturbed by the wildest dreams. I thought I saw Elizabeth, in the bloom of health, walking in the streets of Ingolstadt. Delighted and surprised, I embraced her, but as I imprinted the first kiss on her lips, they became livid with the hue of death; her features appeared to change, and I thought that I held the corpse of my dead mother in my arms; a shroud enveloped her form, and I saw the grave-worms crawling in the folds of the flannel. I started from my sleep with horror; a cold dew covered my forehead, my teeth chattered, and every limb became convulsed; when, by the dim and yellow light of the moon, as it forced its way through the window shutters, I beheld the wretch – the miserable monster whom I had created. He held up the curtain of the bed; and his eyes, if eyes they may be called, were fixed on me. His jaws opened, and he muttered some inarticulate sounds, while a grin wrinkled his cheeks. He might have spoken, but I did not hear; one hand was stretched out, seemingly to detain me, but I escaped and rushed downstairs. I took refuge in the courtyard belonging to the house which I inhabited, where I remained during the rest of the night, walking up and down in the greatest agitation, listening attentively, catching and fearing each sound as if it were to announce the approach of the demoniacal corpse to which I had so miserably given life.

And thus the monster sets out on a murderous rampage, his principal rage being directed at his creator. The novelist is more interested in the moral aspects of the tale than were the makers of the original film—and the dozens of sequels and parodies that have followed. Can anyone forget the ridiculous scene from *Young Frankenstein* where Mel Brooks does a dance routine with the monster to the tune of "Puttin' on the Ritz"?

In spite of the parodies and its age, the film can still mesmerize and chill. Take the opening scene:

We see a dark and foggy cemetery and a gravedigger filling in a grave. Watching from behind the gate are Dr. Victor Frankenstein and his faithful servant, Fritz. In a few moments the gravedigger is gone, and the two are digging up the deceased. As the doctor sort of hugs the coffin, he declares with a true scientist's excited zeal: "He's just resting, waiting for a new life to come!"

Good line—good scene!

℘ ❖ ℧

ANYONE INTERESTED IN WRITING HORROR STORIES MUST READ THE daddy of all horror writers, Edgar Allan Poe. His "A Case of Amontillado" and "The Fall of the House of Usher" have been admired and imitated since they were first written.

His "The Tell-Tale Heart," written in 1843, is a tour de force, a masterful study of a psychotic murderer told in one short soliloquy.

True!—nervous—very, very dreadfully nervous I had been and am! But why *will* you say that I am mad? The disease had sharpened my senses—not destroyed—not dulled them. Above all was the sense of hearing acute. I heard all things in the heaven and in the earth. I heard many things in hell. How, then, am I mad? Hearken! and observe how healthily—how calmly I can tell you the whole story.

It is impossible to tell how first the idea entered my brain; but once conceived, it haunted me day and night. Object there was none. Passion there was none. I loved the old man. He had never wronged me. He had never given me insult. For his gold I had no desire. I think it was his eye! Yes, it was this! One of his eyes resembled that of a vulture—a pale blue eye, with a film over it. Whenever it fell upon me, my blood ran cold; and so by degrees—very gradually—I made up my mind to take the life of the old man, and thus rid myself of the eye forever.

Now this is the point. You fancy me mad. Madmen know nothing. But you should have seen *me*. You should have seen how wisely I proceeded—with what caution—with what fore-sight—with what dissimulation I went to work!

I was never kinder to the old man than during the whole week before I killed him. And every night, about midnight, I turned the latch of his door and opened it—oh, so gently! And then, when I had made an opening sufficient for my head, I put in a dark lantern, all closed, closed, so that no light shone out, and then I thrust in my head. Oh, you would have laughed to see how cunningly I thrust it in! I moved it slowly—very, very slowly, so that I might not disturb the old man's sleep. It took me an hour to place my whole head within the opening so far that I could see him as he lay upon his bed. Ha!—would a madman have been so wise as this? And then, when my head was well in the room, I undid the lantern cautiously—oh, so cautiously—cautiously (for the hinges creaked)—I undid it just so much that a single thin ray fell upon the vulture eye. And this I did for seven long nights—every night just at midnight—but I found the eye always closed; and so it was impossible to do the work; for it was not the old man who vexed me, but his Evil Eye. And every morning, when the day broke, I went boldly into the chamber, and spoke courageously to him, calling him by name in a hearty tone, and inquiring how he had passed the night. So you see he would have been a very profound old man, indeed, to suspect that every night, just at twelve, I looked in upon him while he slept.

Upon the eighth night I was more than usually cautious in opening the door. A watch's minute hand moves more quickly than did mine. Never before that night had I *felt* the extent of my own powers—of my sagacity. I could scarcely contain my feelings of triumph. To think that there I was, opening the door, little by little, and he not even to dream of my secret deeds or thoughts. I fairly chuckled at the idea; and perhaps he heard me; for he moved on the bed suddenly, as if startled. Now you may think that I drew back—but no. His room was as black as pitch with the thick darkness (for the shutters were close fas-tened, through fear of robbers), and so I knew that he could not see the opening of the door, and I kept pushing it on steadily, steadily.

> I had my head in, and was about to open the lantern, when my thumb slipped upon the tin fastening, and the old man sprang up in bed, crying out: "Who's there?"

How effective it is for the character to declare that he is sane! It makes him all the crazier as the tension develops, and he repeatedly congratulates himself on his cleverness.

He kills the old man and buries the dismembered body beneath the floor in his room. While the police are investigating he begins to hear the heartbeats of his victim, louder and louder, and finally in a frenzy, he confesses to the police. When the body is recovered, the murdered man's watch is found to be ticking.

It is generally agreed that Poe's "The Murders in the Rue Morgue," written in 1841, is the genesis of what became the modern mystery genre, complete with the obligatory canny detective who solves the crime.

A mother and daughter are found horribly murdered in their third-floor Paris apartment. The most baffling element is that the door is locked from inside and the window closed—how could the murderer have accomplished this?

Enter the brilliant detective, Auguste Dupin, who solves the case. It seems that a sailor has a pet Ourang-Outang, and it becomes obstreperous, runs away, and climbs up a lightning-rod into an apartment. The sailor follows the ape.

> A lightning-rod is ascended without difficulty, especially by a sailor; but when he had arrived as high as the window, which lay far to his left, his career was stopped; the most that he could accomplish was to reach over so as to obtain a glimpse of the interior of the room. At this glimpse he nearly fell from his hold through excess of horror. Now it was that those hideous shrieks arose upon the night, which had startled from slumber the inmates of the Rue Morgue. Madame L'Espanaye and her daughter, habited in their night clothes, had apparently been occupied in arranging some papers in the iron chest already mentioned, which had been wheeled into the middle of the room. It was open, and its contents lay beside it on the floor. The victims must have been sitting with their backs toward the window; and, from the time elapsing between the ingress of the

beast and the screams, it seems probable that it was not immediately perceived. The flapping-to of the shutter would naturally have been attributed to the wind.

As the sailor looked in, the gigantic animal had seized Madame L'Espanaye by the hair, (which was loose, as she had been combing it,) and was flourishing the razor about her face, in imitation of the motions of a barber. The daughter lay prostrate and motionless; she had swooned. The screams and struggles of the old lady (during which the hair was torn from her head) had the effect of changing the probably pacific purposes of the Ourang-Outang into those of wrath. With one determined sweep of its muscular arm it nearly severed her head from her body. The sight of blood inflamed its anger into phrenzy. Gnashing its teeth, and flashing fire from its eyes, it flew upon the body of the girl, and imbedded its fearful talons in her throat, retaining its grasp until she expired. Its wandering and wild glances fell at this moment upon the head of the bed, over which the face of its master, rigid with horror, was just discernible. The fury of the beast, who no doubt bore still in mind the dreaded whip, was instantly converted into fear. Conscious of having deserved punishment, it seemed desirous of concealing its bloody deeds, and skipped about the chamber in an agony of nervous agitation; throwing down and breaking the furniture as it moved, and dragging the bed from the bedstead. In conclusion, it seized first the corpse of the daughter, and thrust it up the chimney, as it was found; then that of the old lady, which it immediately hurled through the window headlong.

As the ape approached the casement with its mutilated burden, the sailor shrank aghast to the rod, and, rather gliding than clambering down it, hurried at once home—dreading the consequences of the butchery, and gladly abandoning, in his terror, all solicitude about the fate of the Ourang-Outang. The words heard by the party upon the staircase were the Frenchman's exclamations of horror and affright, commingled with the fiendish jabberings of the brute.

I have scarcely anything to add. The Ourang-Outang must have escaped from the chamber, by the rod, just before the breaking of the door.

★ ❖ ★

"The Monkey's Paw," a story written in 1930 by W. W. Jacobs, is one of those classics that every writer of short stories should read—it has endured as one of the best horror tales ever written.

Mr. and Mrs. White, an ordinary English couple with one beloved son, come across and acquire a mummified monkey's paw in an antique shop which they are told has amazing powers: it will grant the owner three wishes. Bemused, the Whites scoff at the claim, but then later, needing money to clear the mortgage on their modest house, and almost in fun, Mr. White asks the paw for 200 pounds. A few days later a gentleman calls at the house with terrible news: their son has been killed at the factory where he worked, horribly mangled by some machinery. The company is extremely sorry and offers the Whites their profound sympathy—and 200 pounds in compensation.

The Whites are terribly shaken up and barely get through the funeral. Then Mrs. White becomes obsessed with an idea: there are two more wishes left on the magic paw! She demands that he ask for their son to come back to life. He refuses; he is afraid. He knows the ghastly extent of the youth's injuries. But she insists.

The final scene:

"Wish!" she cried, in a strong voice.

"It is foolish and wicked," he faltered.

"Wish!" repeated his wife.

He raised his hand. "I wish my son alive again."

The talisman fell to the floor, and he regarded it shudderingly. Then he sank trembling into a chair as the old woman, with burning eyes, walked to the window and raised the blind.

He sat until he was chilled with the cold, glancing occasionally at the figure of the old woman peering through the window. The candle end, which had burnt below the rim of the china candlestick, was throwing pulsating shadows on the ceiling and walls, until, with a flicker larger than the rest, it expired. The old man, with an unspeakable sense of relief at the failure of the talisman, crept back to his bed, and a minute or two afterward the old woman came silently and apathetically beside him.

Neither spoke, but both lay silently listening to the ticking of the clock. A stair creaked, and a squeaky mouse scurried noisily through the wall. The darkness was oppressive, and after lying for some time screwing up his courage, the husband took the box of matches, and striking one, went downstairs for a candle.

At the foot of the stairs the match went out, and he paused to strike another, and at the same moment a knock, so quiet and stealthy as to be scarcely audible, sounded on the front door.

The matches fell from his hand. He stood motionless, his breath suspended until the knock was repeated. Then he turned and fled swiftly back to his room, and closed the door behind him. A third knock sounded through the house.

"What's that?" cried the old woman, starting up.

"A rat," said the old man, in shaking tones—"a rat. It passed me on the stairs."

His wife sat up in bed listening. A loud knock resounded through the house.

"It's Herbert!" she screamed. "It's Herbert!"

She ran to the door, but her husband was before her, and catching her by the arm, held her tightly.

"What are you going to do?" he whispered hoarsely.

"It's my boy; it's Herbert!" she cried, struggling mechanically. "I forgot it was two miles away. What are you holding me for? Let go. I must open the door."

"For God's sake don't let it in," cried the old man, trembling.

"You're afraid of your own son," she cried, struggling. "Let me go. I'm coming, Herbert; I'm coming."

There was another knock, and another. The old woman with a sudden wrench broke free and ran from the room. Her husband followed to the landing, and called after her appealingly as she hurried downstairs. He heard the chain rattle back and the bottom bolt drawn slowly and stiffly from the socket. Then the old woman's voice, strained and panting.

"The bolt," she cried loudly. "Come down. I can't reach it."

But her husband was on his hands and knees groping wildly on the floor in search of the paw. If he could only find it before the thing outside got in. A perfect fusillade of knocks reverberated through the house, and he heard the scraping of a chair as his wife put it down in the passage against the door. He heard the creaking of the bolt as it came slowly back, and at the same moment he found the monkey's paw, and frantically breathed his third and last wish.

The knocking ceased suddenly, although the echoes of it were still in the house. He heard the chair drawn back and the door opened. A cold wind rushed up the staircase, and a long loud wail of disappointment and misery from his wife gave him courage to run down to her side, and then to the gate beyond. The street lamp flickering opposite shone on a quiet and deserted road.

And there you have it—the ultimate be-careful-what-you-wish-for story.

The story would have merely been an anecdotal horror tale of the type told around Boy Scouts' campfires, were it not so credibly written by a master writer.

William Wymark Jacobs died in England in 1943 at the age of eighty, and no one reads anything else of his except "The Monkey's Paw." Such is the fate of many a writer. My mentor, Sinclair Lewis, wrote to me after the publication of my first and forgettable novel, *The Innocent Villa*:

"Just remember," he warned, "the world is filled with writers who have written one book or one story."

෨ ❖ ෬

THE FIRST SHORT STORY I EVER SOLD WAS TO *ESQUIRE*, AND IT WAS based almost literally on a nightmare that I had; I wrote the happenings down the moment I woke up from it. It dealt with a strange band of men and women, a surreal group hired to invade a home in order to drive the unstable owner mad for his money. Unfortunately, that kind of experience has never happened since.

In 1886 Robert Louis Stevenson also had a nightmare. He then wrote a thirty-thousand-word version of it in the amazingly short time of three days. He showed it to his astute wife who criticized it harshly, saying the author had "sacrificed the allegory for magnificent sensationalism."

Stevenson burned the manuscript, realizing she was right. But he set to work again, and three days later appeared with another thirty-thousand-word version.

The Strange Case of Dr. Jekyll and Mr. Hyde became a classic almost instantly, and the names of the protagonist and his evil alter ego have passed into the language.

Many people have conjectured that Stevenson was writing about his alcoholic father who became a different person when he drank alcohol. Whatever the inspiration, until this story no one had written in English about the good and evil that can reside in the same person.

The work was filmed first as a silent in 1920, starring John Barrymore, and many versions have been made since, all making the most of the scene where the doctor mixes his potion and, before our eyes—due to trick photography and clever make-up—becomes the horrendous monster, Mr. Hyde. Perhaps the finest film was the 1932 version starring Frederic March. Before our eyes, using the then new stop-motion technique, we saw the actor's nose and lips coarsen, hair sprout all over his face, fangs appear to grow, and his whole demeanor become more ape-like.

Stevenson's prose account of the transformation of Hyde back to the good Dr. Jekyll near the end of the tale seems less horrendous than the films', showing the reverse process in the beginning of the story.

> He put the glass to his lips, and drank at one gulp. A cry followed; he reeled, staggered, clutched at the table, and held on, staring with injected eyes, gasping with open mouth; and, as I looked, there came, I thought, a change; he seemed to swell; his face became suddenly black, and the features seemed to melt and alter—and the next moment I had sprung to my feet and leaped back against the wall, my arm raised to shield me from that prodigy, my mind submerged in terror.
>
> "O God!" I screamed, and "O God!" again and again; for there before my eyes—pale and shaking, and half fainting, and groping before him with his hands, like a man restored from death—there stood Henry Jekyll!
>
> What he told me in the next hour I cannot bring my mind

to set on paper. I saw what I saw, I heard what I heard, and my soul sickened at it; and yet now, when that sight has faded from my eyes, I ask myself if I believe it, and I cannot answer. My life is shaken to its roots; sleep has left me; the deadliest terror sits by me at all hours of the day and night; I feel that my days are numbered, and that I must die; and yet I shall die incredulous. As for the moral turpitude that man unveiled to me, even with tears of penitence, I cannot, even in memory, dwell on it without a start of horror. I will say but one thing, Utterson, and that (if you can bring your mind to credit it) will be more than enough. The creature who crept into my house that night was, on Jekyll's own confession, known by the name of Hyde, and hunted for in every corner of the land as the murderer of Carew.

᠍᠍ ❖ ᠍

SOMEHOW ONE ISN'T QUITE PREPARED FOR THE LAST SCENE OF SHIRLEY Jackson's "The Lottery," the famous short story that shocked readers of the *New Yorker* magazine in 1948.

The protagonist, Mrs. Hutchinson, lives in a nice "normal" New England village. The townspeople have an annual lottery after which the owner of the losing ticket is ritually killed. Weird and unsettling, the folksy first part changes to this at the end:

> Bill Hutchinson went over to his wife and forced the slip of paper out of her hand. It had a black spot on it, the black spot Mr. Summers had made the night before with the heavy pencil in the coal-company office. Bill Hutchinson held it up, and there was a stir in the crowd.
>
> "All right, folks," Mr. Summers said. "Let's finish quickly."
>
> Although the villagers had forgotten the ritual and lost the original black box, they still remembered to use stones. The pile of stones the boys had made earlier was ready; there were stones on the ground with the blowing scraps of paper that had come out of the box. Mrs. Delacroix selected a stone so large she had to pick it up with both hands and turned to Mrs. Dunbar. "Come on," she said. "Hurry up."
>
> Mrs. Dunbar had small stones in both hands, and she said,

gasping for breath, "I can't run at all. You'll have to go ahead and I'll catch up with you."

The children had stones already, and someone gave little Davy Hutchinson a few pebbles.

Tessie Hutchinson was in the center of a cleared space by now, and she held her hands out desperately as the villagers moved in on her. "It isn't fair," she said. A stone hit her on the side of the head.

Old Man Warner was saying, "Come on, come on, everyone." Steve Adams was in the front of the crowd of villagers, with Mrs. Graves besides him.

"It isn't fair, it isn't right," Mrs. Hutchinson screamed, and then they were upon her.

Countless reams of paper have been covered with theories of what the story means—no two alike, and the author wasn't about to explain.

৪৩ ❖ ೞ

A BAD JOKE IN HOLLYWOOD FOR YEARS HAS BEEN THE LINE: "THE ambitious would-be actress was so dumb that she slept with the writer!"

People tend to forget, especially in Hollywood, that it all begins on a blank page—even visual effects like crashing chandeliers in opera houses. Somewhere, at sometime, a writer dreamed that up.

The *Phantom of the Opera* is so long associated with film—and more recently with the musical—that one forgets that it was once a very popular novel.

Published in 1911, Gaston Leroux's tale is convoluted and, though the characters are the same, little else is in the theatrical version.

The crash to the stage of the great chandelier as is done in both film and theater versions is certainly a never-to-be-forgotten scene, and it comes from the book, but perhaps the most dramatic is the famous unmasking scene. The first, and still perhaps the most horrific, was Lon Chaney's hideous, almost surreal, face in the 1925 silent film. The next version, in 1943, had Susanna Foster ripping off Claude Rains' mask, and it was perhaps more shocking because while equally as horrifying as Chaney's, the ghastly face was less other-worldly.

In the most recent, and tamest, of the dozen versions, the

Andrew Lloyd Webber film version, has Christine (Emmy Rossum) ripping off the reputed monster's mask. What we see, to our great disappointment, is the face of a youngish man (Gerald Butler) with nothing
more scary than what looks like a slightly drooping left eyelid and a
severe case of acne.

Instead of *Ooh! Ugh!* and *Eeuw!* – there comes a surprising feeling
of: *Aw-w-w-w-* ...

Which isn't what Gaston Leroux had in mind when creating his
deranged monster.

Here is how he wrote it. Christine is telling her boyfriend, Raoul,
about the incident with her captor, Erik, the Phantom:

> She took Raoul's protecting hands in hers and, with a long
> shiver, continued:
> "Yes, if I lived to be a hundred, I should always hear the
> superhuman cry of grief and rage which he uttered when the
> terrible sight appeared before my eyes...."

She goes on:

> "I fell back against the wall and he came up to me, grind-
> ing his teeth, and, as I fell upon my knees, he hissed mad, inco-
> herent words and curses at me. Leaning over me, he cried, 'Look!
> You want to see! See! Feast your eyes, glut your soul on my
> cursed ugliness! Look at Erik's face! Now you know the face of
> the voice! You were not content to hear me, eh? You wanted to
> know what I looked like! Oh, you women are so inquisitive!
> Well, are you satisfied? I'm a very good-looking fellow,
> eh?...When a woman has seen me, as you have, she belongs to
> me. She loves me for ever. I am a kind of Don Juan, you know!'
> And, drawing himself up to his full height, with his hand on his
> hip, wagging the hideous thing that was his head on his shoul-
> ders, he roared, 'Look at me! *I am Don Juan triumphant!* And,
> when I turned away my head and begged for mercy, he drew it
> to him, brutally, twisting his dead fingers into my hair."
> "Enough! Enough!" cried Raoul. "I will kill him. In
> Heaven's name, Christine, tell me where the dining-room on
> the lake is! I must kill him!"

"Oh, be quiet, Raoul, if you want to know!"

"Yes, I want to know how and why you went back; I must know!...But, in any case, I will kill him!"

"Oh, Raoul, listen, listen!...He dragged me by my hair and then...and then...Oh, it is too horrible!"

"Well, what? Out with it!" exclaimed Raoul fiercely. "Out with it, quick!"

"Then he hissed at me. 'Ah, I frighten you, do I?...I dare say!...Perhaps you think that I have another mask, eh, and that this...this...my head is a mask? Well,' he roared, 'tear it off as you did the other! Come! Come along! I insist! Your hands! Your hands! Give me your hands!' And he seized my hands and dug them into his awful face. He tore his flesh with my nails, tore his terrible dead flesh with my nails!...'Know,' he shouted, while his throat throbbed and panted like a furnace, 'know that I am built up of death from head to foot and that it is a corpse that loves you and adores you and will never, never leave you!...Look, I am not laughing now, I am crying, crying for you, Christine, who have torn off my mask and who therefore can never leave me again!...As long as you thought me handsome, you could have come back, I know you would have come back...but, now that you know my hideousness, you would run away for good...So I shall keep you here!...Why did you want to see me?...When my own father never saw me and when my mother, so as not to see me, made me a present of my first mask!'

"He had let go of me at last and was dragging himself about on the floor, uttering terrible sobs. And then he crawled away like a snake, went into his room, closed the door and left me alone to my reflections. Presently I heard the sound of the organ; and then I began to understand Erik's contemptuous phrase when he spoke about opera music. What I now heard was utterly different from what I had heard up to then. His *Don Juan Triumphant* (for I had no doubt but that he had rushed to his masterpiece to forget the horror of the moment) seemed to me at first one long, awful, magnificent sob. But, little by little, it expressed every emotion, every suffering of which mankind is capable. It intoxicated me; and I opened the door that separated us. Erik rose, as I entered, *but dared not turn in my direction.* 'Erik,' I cried, 'show me your face without fear! I swear that you are the most unhappy and sublime of men; and, if ever again I shiver when I look at you, it will be because I am thinking of the splendor of your genius!' Then Erik turned round, for he believed me, and I also had faith in myself. He fell at my feet, with words of love…with words of love in his dead mouth…and the music had ceased…He kissed the hem of my dress and did not see that I closed my eyes."

ॐ ❖ ॐ

Oscar Wilde's period novel, *The Picture of Dorian Gray*, created a sensation when it was first published in 1891. Though fraught with moral judgments and homosexual undertones, what are remembered about the story are two dramatic scenes.

Basil Hallward, a fine portrait artist in London, is captivated by a twenty-year-old man named Dorian Gray, whose physical beauty is beyond belief. He paints the Adonis life-size, and when Dorian sees his likeness on canvas he says he would give his soul to remain so youthfully handsome. He takes the painting home. Subsequently, after he has acted cruelly to a woman, he notices that the portrait has altered slightly, and not for the good. He retires the picture to an upstairs locked room and pursues a hedonistic life of opium, debauchery, and crime.

When Dorian is thirty-eight, the painter, Basil, visits him to persuade him to change his way of life. Dorian physically remains as young and handsome as ever, but when Basil insists on seeing the portrait that he has painted eighteen years ago, here is the scene that ensues:

"So you think that it is only God who sees the soul, Basil? Draw that curtain back, and you will see mine."

The voice that spoke was cold and cruel. "You are mad, Dorian, or playing a part," muttered Hallward, frowning.

"You won't? Then I must do it myself," said the young man; and he tore the curtain from its rod, and flung it on the ground.

An exclamation of horror broke from the painter's lips as he saw in the dim light the hideous face on the canvas grinning at him. There was something in its expression that filled him with disgust and loathing. Good heavens! It was Dorian Gray's own face that he was looking at! The horror, whatever it was, had not yet entirely spoiled that marvelous beauty. There was still some gold in the thinning hair and some scarlet on the sensual mouth. The sodden eyes had kept something of the loveliness of their blue, the noble curves had not yet completely passed away from chiseled nostrils and from plastic throat. Yes, it was Dorian himself. But who had done it? He seemed to recognize his own brush-work, and the frame was his own design. The idea was monstrous, yet he felt afraid. He seized the lighted candle, and held it to the picture. In the left-hand corner was his own name, traced in long letters of bright vermilion.

Dorian stabs the painter to death and finds a way to dispose of the body. A few weeks later he looks at the painting and, to his horror, discovers that blood is depicted on one of the hands. Here are the final scenes of the novel:

He looked round, and saw the knife that had stabbed Basil Hallward. He had cleaned it many times, till there was no stain left upon it. It was bright, and glistened. As it had killed the painter, so it would kill the painter's work, and all that that meant. It would kill the past, and when that was dead he would be free. It would kill this monstrous soul-life, and, without its hideous warnings, he would be at peace. He seized the thing, and stabbed the picture with it.

There was a cry heard, and a crash. The cry was so horrible in its agony that the frightened servants woke, and crept out of their rooms. Two gentlemen, who were passing in the Square below, stopped, and looked up at the great house. They walked on till they met a policeman, and brought him back. The man rang the bell several times, but there was no answer. Except for a light in one of the top windows, the house was all dark. After a time, he went away and stood in an adjoining portico and watched.

"Whose house is that, constable?" asked the elder of the two gentlemen.

"Mr. Dorian Gray's, sir," answered the policeman.

They looked at each other, as they walked away, and sneered. One of them was Sir Henry Ashton's uncle.

Inside, in the servants' part of the house, the half-clad domestics were talking in low whispers to each other. Old Mrs. Leaf was crying and wringing her hands. Francis was as pale as death.

After about a quarter of an hour, he got the coachman and one of the footmen and crept upstairs. They knocked, but there was no reply. They called out. Everything was still. Finally, after vainly trying to force the door, they got on the roof, and dropped down on to the balcony. The windows yielded easily: their bolts were old.

When they entered they found, hanging upon the wall, a splendid portrait of their master as they had last seen him, in all the wonder of his exquisite youth and beauty. Lying on the floor was a dead man, in evening dress, with a knife in his heart. He was withered, wrinkled, and loathsome of visage. It was not till they had examined the rings that they recognized who it was.

Naturally, the 1945 film, starring Hurd Hatfield, George Sanders, and Angela Lansbury, took full advantage of the graphic drama of these two scenes.

In 1895, just four years after the publication of *Dorian Gray*, Wilde was convicted of homosexual practices and was sentenced to two years of hard labor in prison. Upon release, physically, spiritually, and financially ruined, he moved to Paris for his three final years, "dying as I lived, beyond my means."

෨ ❖ ෬

ONE CERTAINLY EXPECTS *DRAMATIC* SCENES IN A MARIO PUZO NOVEL but not necessarily *horror* scenes.

The beginning writer can learn a great deal by reading and studying the many fine scenes in *The Godfather*:

Sonny and the maid of honor upstairs in the raunchy scene at the wedding party; the early one where the Don growls out the immortal phrase "make him an offer he can't refuse"; the carefully crafted killing by Michael of the police captain in the restaurant; the tender scene where the Godfather is playing in the garden with his grandson and has a heart attack

—et alia!

But! What scene in both the book and the 1972 Francis Coppola film will you never forget? The horror scene.

Jack Woltz (played by John Marley) is a big-shot arrogant Hollywood producer who has unwisely defied the mafia and said he would never give the plum role in his new movie to the Godfather's singer-turned-actor godson, Johnny Fontane. Somehow Woltz must be convinced. Tom Hagen, the Godfather's right-hand man, learns that the only thing Woltz truly loves or cares about is his famous race horse, Khartoum; Hagen takes action, and this is the result:

> 66 Like sex and romance technique, the writing of horror stories is a very individual thing as is a reader's choice of them. 99

Jack Woltz always slept alone. He had a bed big enough for ten people and a bedroom large enough for a movie ballroom scene, but he had slept alone since the death of his first wife ten years before. This did not mean he no longer used women. He was physically a vigorous man despite his age, but he could be aroused now only by very young girls and had learned that a few hours in the evening were all the youth of his body and his patience could tolerate.

On this Thursday morning, for some reason, he awoke early. The light of dawn made his huge bedroom as misty as a foggy meadowland. Far down at the foot of his bed was a familiar shape and Woltz struggled up on his elbows to get a clearer look. It had the shape of a horse's head. Still groggy, Woltz reached and flicked on the night table lamp.

The shock of what he saw made him physically ill. It seemed as if a great sledgehammer had struck him on the chest, his heartbeat jumped erratically and he became nauseous. His vomit spluttered on the thick flair rug.

Severed from its body, the black silky head of the great horse Khartoum was stuck fast in a thick cake of blood. White, reedy tendons showed. Froth covered the muzzle and those apple-sized eyes that had glinted like gold were mottled the color of rotting fruit with dead, hemorrhaged blood. Woltz was struck by a purely animal terror and out of that terror he screamed for his servants and out of that terror he called Hagen to make his uncontrolled threats. His maniacal raving alarmed the butler, who called Woltz's personal physician and his second in command at the studio.

Here is a splendid example of "show—don't tell": a beginning writer might have had Woltz be "horrified and terrified" at the sight of his beloved horse's head, but Puzo does not *tell* us that, he *shows* us graphically what Woltz's reaction is.

Quite naturally, Johnny Fontane gets the part.

Hollywood rumors suggested that this section of the novel was based on Frank Sinatra's career and his desperate desire to get the part of the ill-fated soldier, Maggio, in *From Here to Eternity* (for which he earned a best supporting Oscar).

ℬ ❖ ℭ

"A ROSE FOR EMILY" BY WILLIAM FAULKNER IS A STORY THAT every would-be writer of short stories should know. It is a terse, no-nonsense, old-fashioned great story that somehow doesn't seem like a Faulkner story, perhaps because of the chilling and all-revealing last scene.

An eccentric woman in the South, jilted by her lover, becomes a recluse in her mansion. The author gives us a slight clue when Miss Emily buys some rat poison early in the story, but we don't have all the information until the end—the *very* end, after her funeral:

Already we knew that there was one room in that region above stairs which no one had seen in forty years, and which would have to be forced. They waited until Miss Emily was decently in the ground before they opened it.

The violence of breaking down the door seemed to fill this room with pervading dust. A thin, acrid pall as of the tomb seemed to lie everywhere upon this room decked and furnished as for a bridal: upon the valence curtains of faded rose color, upon the rose-shaded lights, upon the dressing table, upon the delicate array of crystal and the man's toilet things backed with tarnished silver, silver so tarnished that the monogram was obscured. Among them lay a collar and tie, as if they had just been removed, which, lifted, left upon the surface a pale crescent in the dust. Upon a chair hung the suit, carefully folded; beneath it the two mute shoes and the discarded socks.

The man himself lay in the bed.

For a long while we just stood there, looking down at the profound and fleshless grin. The body had apparently once lain in the attitude of an embrace, but now the long sleep that outlasts love, that conquers even the grimace of love, had cuckolded him. What was left of him, rotted beneath what was left of the nightshirt, had become inextricable from the bed in which he lay; and upon him and upon the pillow beside him lay that even coating of the patient and biding dust.

Then we noticed that in the second pillow was the indentation of a head. One of us lifted something from it, and leaning forward, that faint and invisible dust dry and acrid in the nostrils, we saw a long strand of iron-gray hair.

Like sex and romance technique, the writing of horror stories is a very individual thing as is a reader's choice of them. Some like their stories as real as possible, like Jack Nicholson's sinister "Heeere's Johnny!" killer in *The Shining*. Others gravitate to the more metaphysical like the stories of Dean Koontz and Matt Pallamary and sometimes the protean Stephen King. The master of the genre, E. A. Poe, is very realistic. And there's Patricia Cornwell's horrors of the autopsy room.

In any case, one should read extensively in the genre before attempting it.

12

Juveniles

RUDYARD KIPLING WAS ONE OF THE MOST POPULAR WRITERS England has produced, and perhaps his books and stories for and about children are his greatest legacy: *Kim*, the two *The Jungle Books*, and *Just So Stories*.

Just So Stories, 1903, the only book Kipling illustrated himself, contains such tall stories as "How the Elephant Got Its Trunk" and, best of all, the moving "Rikki-Tikki-Tavi" tale.

It is the story of a brave and lovable young mongoose (told from his point of view), who is saved by an English boy, Teddy, who lives in India with his parents. Rikki becomes a beloved pet of the family and once saves Teddy from a small poisonous snake. But it is the fierce big cobra, Nag, who intends to kill the whole family that Rikki most worries about. Here is the scene of the inevitable encounter, and there are several things to be learned from this simple tale written by a master storyteller.

The villainous Nag has slunk into the bathroom of the family, awaiting the awakening of the family in the morning. The snake figures that after he kills the humans, the mongoose will also leave.

Nag coiled himself down, coil by coil, round the bulge at the bottom of the water-jar, and Rikki-tikki stayed still as death. After an hour he began to move, muscle by muscle, towards the jar. Nag was asleep, and Rikki-tikki looked at his big back, wondering which would be the best place for a good hold. "If I don't break his back at the first jump," said Rikki, "he can still fight; and if he fights—oh, Rikki!" He looked at the thickness of the neck below the hood, but that was too much for him; and a bite near the tail would only make Nag savage.

"It must be the head," he said at last; "the head above the hood; and when I am once there, I must not let go."

Then he jumped. The head was lying a little clear of the water-jar, under the curve of it; and, as his teeth met, Rikki braced his back against the bulge of the red earthenware to hold down the head. This gave him just one second's purchase, and he made the most of it. Then he was battered to and fro as a rat is shaken by a dog—to and fro on the floor, up and down, and round in great circles; but his eyes were red, and he held on as the body cart-whipped over the floor, up-setting the tin dipper and the soap-dish and the flesh-brush, and banged against the tin side of the bath. As he held he closed his jaws tighter and tighter, for he made sure he would be banged to death, and, for the honor of his family, he pre-ferred to be found with his teeth locked. He was dizzy, ach-ing, and felt shaken to pieces when something went off like a thunderclap just behind him; a hot wind knocked him sense-less, and red fire singed his fur. The big man had been wak-ened by the noise, and had fired both barrels of a shot-gun into Nag just behind the hood.

Rikki-tikki held on with his eyes shut, for now he was quite sure he was dead; but the head did not move, and the big man picked him up and said: "It's the mongoose again, Alice; the little chap has saved *our* lives now."

Rikki still must face his greatest challenge—Nag's vicious wife, Nagaina. He destroys her eggs, then does the unthinkable—he follows her down the hole that is her home and by sheer pluck kills her, and the family lives snake-free and happily ever after.

This story, though written for children, employs all the elements that successful writers of adult fiction must be constantly aware of in their stories:

1. We have a likable hero, though only an animal, for whom we are rooting.

2. He has a goal (protecting his master from harm); we want to see him attain that goal very much.

3. **The antagonists (the snakes) who stand in the way of the hero's goal are worthy and dangerous foes.**

4. **It is not easy to attain his goal, but through his character and courage he succeeds.**

5. **The ending is satisfying. It is a happy one in this case, but even if the hero's goal had not been reached, if the ending had been an unhappy one, if the reader understands the whys of the failure, it would be *satisfying* to the reader.**

℘ ❖ ℭ

ALTHOUGH THEORETICALLY A BOOK FOR YOUNG READERS, AND FULL of wonderfully humorous moments, the scenes of Beth's death in *Little Women* made adults of both sexes weep.

Originally titled *The Pathetic Family*, Louisa May Alcott's account of four girls' experiences growing up in an eccentric household was published in 1868 to resounding acclaim, and it is still very popular. (It has been filmed several times, but none equals the first one made in 1933, with a fine cast headed by Katharine Hepburn as the protagonist, Jo.)

The novel is clearly based on the author's life, and the death of the lovely sister, Beth, is based on the actual loss of Louisa's sister in 1858.

In the chapter "The Valley of the Shadow," the desperately ill Beth has come across a lovely farewell poem written about her by Jo.

Blurred and blotted, faulty and feeble, as the lines were, they brought a look of inexpressible comfort to Beth's face, for her one regret had been that she had done so little and this seemed to assure her that her life had not been useless, that her death would not bring the despair she feared. As she sat with the paper folded between her hands, the charred log fell asunder, Jo started up, revived the blaze, and crept to the bedside, hoping Beth slept.

"Not asleep, but so happy, dear. See, I found this and read it; I knew you wouldn't care. Have I been all that to you, Jo?" she asked, with wistful, humble earnestness.

"O Beth, so much, so much!" and Jo's head went down upon the pillow, beside her sister's.

"Then I don't feel as if I'd wasted my life. I'm not so good as you make me, but I *have* tried to do right; and now, when it's too late to begin even to do better, it's such a comfort to know that some one loves me so much, and feels as if I'd helped them."

"More than any one in the world, Beth. I used to think I couldn't let you go; but I'm learning to feel that I don't lose you; that you'll be more to me than ever, and death can't part us, though it seems to."

With great fortitude Beth hangs on to her fragile life.

So the spring days came and went, the sky grew clearer, the earth greener, the flowers were up fair and early, and the birds came back in time to say good-by to Beth, who, like a tired but trustful child, clung to the hands that had led her all her life, as father and mother guided her tenderly through the Valley of the Shadow, and gave her up to God.

Seldom, except in books, do the dying utter memorable words, see visions, or depart with beautified countenances; and those who have sped many parting souls know that to most the end comes as naturally and simply as sleep. As Beth had hoped, the "tide went out easily"; and in the dark hour before the dawn, on the bosom where she had drawn her first breath, she quietly drew her last, with no farewell but one loving look, one little sigh.

With tears and prayers and tender hands, mother and sisters made her ready for the long sleep that pain would never mar again, seeing with grateful eyes the beautiful serenity that soon replaced the pathetic patience that had wrung their hearts so long, and feeling, with reverent joy, that to their darling death was a benignant angel, not a phantom full of dread.

When morning came, for the first time in many months the fire was out, Jo's place was empty, and the room was very still. But a bird sang blithely on a budding bough, close by, the snow-drops blossomed freshly at the window, and the spring sunshine streamed in like a benediction over the placid face upon the pillow—a face so full of painless peace that those who loved it best smiled through their tears, and thanked God that Beth was well at last.

Talk about "aiming for the heart"; it is hard to resist heartfelt lines like: "…for love is the only thing that we can carry with us when we go, and it makes the end so easy."

ℰ ❖ ℐ

ALTHOUGH WRITTEN AS A BITTER AND CAUSTIC SOCIAL SATIRE, AIMED at the English people in general and the Whigs specifically, Jonathan Swift's 1726 fantasy *Gulliver's Travels* has long been treated as a young person's story.

Lemuel Gulliver, a physician, takes a position as ship's doctor on the *Antelope* which sets sail for the South Seas. The original book takes place on three separate voyages and countries—a land of little people, Lilliput; a land of giants; Brobdingnag, and the land of rational horses, the Houyhnhnms. However, the story of the Lilliputians is the best known to children, and here is their favorite scene, which has been reproduced in films and animated cartoons many times.

Gulliver's ship is wrecked, and he takes to a small boat with some other men.

> We therefore trusted ourselves to the Mercy of the Waves; and in about half an Hour the Boat was overset by a sudden Flurry from the North. What became of my Companions in the Boat, as well as of those who escaped on the Rock, or were left in the Vessel, I cannot tell; but conclude they were all lost. For my own Part, I swam as Fortune directed me, and was pushed forward by Wind and Tide. I often let my Legs drop, and could feel no Bottom: But when I was almost gone, and able to struggle no longer, I found myself within my Depth; and by this Time the Storm was much abated. The Declivity was so small, that I walked near a Mile before I got to the Shore, which I conjectured was about Eight o'Clock in the Evening. I then advanced forward near half a Mile, but could not discover any Sign of Houses or Inhabitants; at least I was in so weak a

Condition, that I did not observe them. I was extremely tired, and with that, and the heat of the Weather, and about half a Pint of Brandy that I drank as I left the Ship, I found myself much inclined to sleep. I lay down on the Grass, which was very short and soft; where I slept sounder than ever I remember to have done in my Life, and as I reckoned, about Nine Hours; for when I awaked, it was just Day-light. I attempted to rise, but was not able to stir: For as I happened to lie on my Back, I found my Arms and Legs were strongly fastened on each Side to the Ground; and my Hair, which was long and thick, tied down in the same Manner. I likewise felt several slender Ligatures across my Body, from my Armpits to my Thighs. I could only look upwards; the Sun began to grow hot, and the Light offended my Eyes. I heard a confused Noise about me, but in the Posture I lay, could see nothing except the Sky. In a little time I felt something alive moving on my left Leg, which advancing gently forward over my Breast, came almost up to my Chin; when bending my Eyes downwards as much as I could, I perceived it to be a human Creature not six Inches high, with a Bow and Arrow in his Hands, and a Quiver at his Back. In the mean time, I felt at least Forty more of the same Kind (as I conjectured) following the first. I was in the utmost Astonishment, and roared so loud, that they all ran back in a Fright; and some of them, as I was afterwards told, were hurt with the Falls they got by leaping from my Sides upon the Ground. However, they soon returned; and one of them, who ventured so far as to get a full Sight of my Face, lifting up his Hands and Eyes by way of Admiration, cried out in a shrill, but distinct Voice, *Hekinah Degul*: The others repeated the same Words several times, but I then knew not what they meant. I lay all this while, as the Reader may believe, in great Uneasiness: At length, struggling to get loose, I had the Fortune to break the Strings, and wrench out the Pegs that fastened my left Arm to the Ground; for, by lifting it up to my Face, I discovered the Methods they had taken to bind me; and, at the same time, with a violent Pull, which gave me excessive Pain, I a little loosened the Strings that tied down my Hair on the left Side; so that I was just able to turn my head about two Inches. But the Creatures ran off a second time, before I could seize them; whereupon there was a great Shout in a very shrill Accent; and after it ceased, I heard one of them cry aloud, *Tolgo Phonac*; when in an Instant I felt above an Hundred Arrows discharged on my left Hand, which pricked me like so many Needles; and besides, they shot another Flight into the Air, as we do Bombs in *Europe*; whereof many, I suppose, fell on my Body, (though I felt them not) and some on my Face, which I immediately covered with my left Hand. When this Shower of Arrows was over, I fell a groaning with Grief and Pain; and then striving again to get loose, they discharged another Volley larger than the first; and some of them attempted with Spears to stick me in the Sides; but, by good Luck, I had on me a Buff Jerkin, which they could not pierce. I thought it the most prudent Method to lie still; and my Design was to continue so till Night, when my left Hand being already loose, I could easily free myself: And as for the Inhabitants, I had Reason to believe I might be a Match for the greatest Armies they could bring against me, if they were all of the same Size with him that I saw. But Fortune disposed otherwise of me. When the People observed I was quiet, they discharged no more Arrows.

Gulliver becomes a great friend to the little people and helps them in the war they're engaged in. Swift's wry comment on the stupidity of any war is the reason for this war: it is caused by the Big Enders, who declare that boiled eggs should only be cut open at the big end, against the radical Little Enders, who insist upon the opposite method.

Someone has observed that along with the Trojan War, where both sides were fighting for possession of Helen of Troy, the Lilliputian war is the only other war on record where both sides knew *exactly* what they were fighting about!

℘ ❖ ℞

THERE ARE SO MANY FINE SCENES IN MARK TWAIN'S *TOM SAWYER* that it is hard to pick one—Tom's pirate gang, Jackson's Island, the fake funeral, Injun Joe, the "courtship" of Becky Thatcher, the cave—but first and foremost, the whitewashing of the fence jumps to mind whenever one thinks of Twain's 1876 novel, surely the best boy's book ever written.

Tom's Aunt Polly has ordered him to whitewash the fences, a dreary dreaded task, but he sets to work.

> But Tom's energy did not last. He began to think of the fun he had planned for this day, and his sorrows multiplied. Soon the free boys would come tripping along on all sorts of delicious expeditions, and they would make a world of fun of him for having to work—the very thought of it burnt him like fire. He got out his worldly wealth and examined it—bits of toys, marbles, and trash; enough to buy an exchange of *work*, maybe, but not half enough to buy so much as half an hour of pure freedom. So he returned his straitened means to his pocket and gave up the idea of trying to buy the boys. At this dark and hopeless moment an inspiration burst upon him! Nothing less than a great, magnificent inspiration.
>
> He took up his brush and went tranquilly to work. Ben Rogers hove in sight presently—the very boy, of all boys, whose ridicule he had been dreading

Ben watches Tom a few moments, then scoffs:

> "Hi-*yi! You're* up a stump, ain't you!"
>
> No answer. Tom surveyed his last touch with the eye of an artist, then he gave his brush another gentle sweep and surveyed the result, as before. Ben ranged up alongside of him. Tom's mouth watered for the apple, but he stuck to his work. Ben said:
>
> "Hello, old chap, you got to work, hey?"
>
> Tom wheeled suddenly and said:
>
> "Why, it's you, Ben! I warn't noticing."
>
> "Say—*I'm* going in a'swimming, *I* am. Don't you wish you could? But of course you'd druther *work*—wouldn't you? Course you would!"
>
> Tom contemplated the boy a bit, and said:
>
> "What do you call work?"
>
> "Why, ain't *that* work?"

Tom resumed his whitewashing, and answered carelessly:

"Well maybe it is, and maybe it ain't. All I know is, it suits Tom Sawyer."

"Oh come, now, you don't mean to let on that you *like* it?"

The brush continued to move.

"Like it? Well, I don't see why I oughtn't to like it. Does a boy get a chance to whitewash a fence every day?"

That put the thing in a new light. Ben stopped nibbling his apple. Tom swept his brush daintily back and forth—stepped back to note the effect—added a touch here and there—criticized the effect again—Ben watching every move and getting more and more interested, more and more absorbed. Presently he said:

"Say, Tom, let *me* whitewash a little."

Tom considered, was about to consent; but he altered his mind:

"No—no—I reckon it wouldn't hardly do, Ben. You see, Aunt Polly's awful particular about this fence—right here on the street, you know—but if it was the back fence I wouldn't mind and *she* wouldn't. Yes, she's awful particular about this fence; it's got to be done very careful; I reckon there ain't one boy in a thousand, maybe two thousand, that can do it the way it's got to be done."

"No—is that so? Oh come, now—lemme just try. Only just a little—I'd let *you*, if you was *me*, Tom."

"Ben, I'd like to, honest Injun; but Aunt Polly—well, Jim wanted to do it, but she wouldn't let him; Sid wanted to do it, and she wouldn't let Sid. Now don't you see how I'm fixed? If you was to tackle this fence and anything was to happen to it—"

"Oh, shucks, I'll be just as careful. Now lemme try. Say—I'll give you the core of my apple."

"Well, here—No, Ben, now don't. I'm afeard—"

"I'll give you *all* of it!"

Tom gave up the brush with reluctance in his face, but alacrity in his heart. And while the late steamer *Big Missouri* worked and sweated in the sun, the retired artist sat on a barrel in the shade close by, dangled his legs, munched his apple, and planned the slaughter of more innocents. There was no lack of material; boys happened along every little while; they came to jeer, but remained to whitewash. By the time Ben was fagged out, Tom had traded the next chance to Billy Fisher for a kite, in good repair; and when *he* played out, Johnny Miller bought in for a dead rat and a string to swing it with—and so on, and so on, hour after hour. And when the middle of the afternoon came, from being a poor poverty-stricken boy in the morning, Tom was literally rolling wealth. He had, besides the things before mentioned, twelve marbles, part of a jew's-harp, a piece of blue bottle glass to look through, a spool cannon, a key that wouldn't unlock anything, a fragment of chalk, a glass stopper of a decanter, a tin soldier, a couple of tadpoles, six firecrackers, a kitten with only one eye, a brass doorknob, a dog collar—but no dog—the handle of a knife, four pieces of orange peel, and a dilapidated old window sash.

He had had a nice, good, idle time all the while—plenty of company—and the fence had three coats of whitewash on it! If he hadn't run out of whitewash, he would have bankrupted every boy in the village.

Tom said to himself that it was not such a hollow world, after all. He had discovered a great law of human action, without knowing it—namely, that in order to make a man or a boy covet a thing, it is only necessary to make the thing difficult to attain.

And thus was born one of the great scam artists of all time!

☜ ❖ ☞

WHEN I WAS ABOUT TEN I WAS KNOWN AS THE DEMON PUPPETEER OF Burlingame, California. I made their heads from plastic wood, put their dowel bodies together with screw-eyes, and sewed their costumes. Actually, they were not puppets; they were technically marionettes since they were made to move by strings, rather than gloved hands like Punch and Judy. Pinocchio was a marionette, which is perhaps why I loved the book and the film so much.

One of the most universally loved books by all ages and all countries, *The Adventures of Pinocchio*, was written in 1883 by Carlo Lorenzini, of Florence, Italy, under the pen name of Collodi.

Disney's 1940 animated cartoon feature based on the book is perhaps that studio's finest work. "A joy," wrote critic Leonard Maltin, "no matter how many times you see it."

Scene after scene in the film follows the book's prose exactly as Collodi wrote it. Here is the terrifying scene on the island, where naughty boys who dislike school and want nothing more than to play all day are sent.

This delightful life had gone on for five months. The days had been entirely spent in play and amusement, without a thought of books or school, when one morning Pinocchio awoke to a most disagreeable surprise that, to say the least, put him into a very bad humor.

What was this surprise?

I'll tell you, my dear little readers. The surprise was that Pinocchio when he awoke scratched his head; and in scratching his head he discovered...Can you possibly guess what he discovered?

He discovered to his great astonishment that his ears had grown more than six inches.

The puppet from his birth had such very small ears that they were barely visible to the naked eye. You can imagine, then, what he felt when he found that during the night his ears had become so long that they felt like two brooms.

He went at once in search of a mirror so he could look at himself, but not being able to find one he filled the basin of his washing stand with water, and he saw reflected there what he certainly would never have wished to see. He saw his head decorated with a magnificent pair of donkey's ears!

Think of poor Pinocchio's sorrow, shame, and despair!

He began to cry and roar, and he beat his head against the wall; but the more he cried the longer his ears grew: they grew, and grew, and became hairy toward the points.

At the sound of his loud cries a beautiful little Marmot that lived on the first floor came into the room. Seeing the puppet in such grief, she asked earnestly:

"What's happened to you, my dear fellow lodger?"

"I'm ill, my dear little Marmot, very ill…and of a sickness that frightens me. Do you know how to take a pulse? Maybe I have a fever."

The little Marmot raised her right forepaw; and after having felt Pinocchio's pulse she said to him, sighing:

"My friend, I'm sorry—I have bad news!"

"What is it?"

"You have got a very bad fever!"

"What is it?"

"It is donkey fever."

"A fever that I don't know anything about," said the puppet, but he was beginning to understand it only too well.

"I will explain it to you," said the Marmot. "In two or three hours you will be no longer a puppet, or a boy…"

"What…what shall I be?"

"In two or three hours you'll become really and truly a little donkey, like the ones that pull carts and haul cabbages and lettuce to market."

"Oh, poor me! Poor me!" cried Pinocchio, grabbing his two ears with his hands, and pulling them and tearing them furiously as if they had been someone else's ears.

"My dear boy," said the Marmot, consoling him, "what can you do to prevent it? It is destiny. It is written that all boys who are lazy, and who take a dislike to books, to schools, and to teachers, and who spend their time in amusement, games, and idle play, must end sooner or later by becoming transformed into so many little donkeys."

"Is it really true?" asked the puppet, sobbing.

"Only too true! And tears are now useless. You should have thought of it sooner!"

"Not my fault: believe me, little Marmot, the fault was all Candlewick's!"

"And who is this Candlewick?"

"One of my schoolfellows. I wanted to go home! I wanted to be obedient. I wanted to study and earn a good character…but Candlewick said to me: 'Why should you bother yourself studying? Why go to school? … Come with us instead to the Land of

Boobies! There we'll amuse ourselves from morning to night, and we shall always be merry.'"

"And why did you follow the advice of that false friend—of that bad companion?"

"Why? … Because, my dear little Marmot, I am just a puppet with no sense…and with no heart. Ah, if I had had any I should never have left that good Fairy who loved me like a mother, and who had done so much for me! … And I would no longer be a puppet. By this time I'd have become a little boy like so many others! If I meet Candlewick, woe to him! He shall hear what I think of him!"

He finds Candlewick at his home.

And then a scene followed that would seem incredible if it was not true. When Pinocchio and Candlewick discovered that they were both struck with the same misfortune, instead of feeling full of shame and grief, they began to prick up their ungainly ears and to tear around, and then ended by going into bursts of laughter.

And they laughed, and laughed, and laughed, until they had to hold their sides. But in the midst of their merriment, Candlewick suddenly stopped, staggered, and said to his friend:

"Help, help, Pinocchio!"

"What's the matter with you?"

"I can't stand up straight!"

"Neither can I!" exclaimed Pinocchio, tottering and beginning to cry.

And while they were talking they both doubled up and began to run around the room on their hands and feet. And as they ran, their hands became hoofs, their faces lengthened into muzzles, and their backs became covered with a light-gray hairy coat sprinkled with black.

But do you know what was the worst moment for those two wretched boys? The worst and the most humiliating moment was when their tails grew! Overcome by shame and sorrow, they wept and lamented their fate.

Oh, if they had but been wiser! But instead of sighs and

lamentations they could only bray like asses; and they brayed loudly and said in chorus: "Eeeh-or, eeeh-or, eeeh-or!"

But, like all good fairy stories, this one ends happily—after his terrible session as a cart donkey, Pinocchio mends his ways, gets back home, tells no more nose-growing fibs, and is made into a real boy by the fairy to the delight of his carpenter "father" Gepetto.

ಬ ❖ ಐ

PERHAPS THE MOST MOVING AND DRAMATIC SCENE IN THE IMMORTAL film *The Wizard of Oz* (which should receive a special Oscar for a "film that parents don't mind seeing a tenth time with their children") appears near the end of the movie.

Sometimes, and not all that rarely, the moving picture version of a great work is better than the book. The brief, lovely, and poignant scene when Judy Garland as Dorothy Gale, and Frank Morgan, as the fraudulent wizard, face the fact that his effects have only been mechanical and that he is a fraud is in contrast with the verbose and lengthy scene in Frank L. Baum's 1900 *The Wonderful Wizard of Oz*.

Here's the unmasking scene in the book which occurs when Dorothy and her pals decide to go to the throne room and confront the wizard for failing to fulfill his promises.

> They kept close to the door and closer to one another, for the stillness of the empty room was more dreadful than any of the forms they had seen Oz take.
>
> Presently they heard a Voice, seeming to come from somewhere near the top of the great dome, and it said solemnly:
>
> "I am Oz, the Great and Terrible. Why do you seek me?"
>
> They looked again in every part of the room and then, seeing no one, Dorothy asked: "Where are you?"
>
> "I am everywhere," answered the voice, "but to the eyes of common mortals I am invisible. I will now seat myself upon my throne, that you may converse with me." Indeed the Voice seemed just then to come straight from the throne itself; so they walked toward it and stood in a row, while Dorothy said: "We have come to claim our promise, O Oz."

"What promise?" asked Oz.

"You promised to send me back to Kansas when the Wicked Witch was destroyed," said the girl.

"And you promised to give me brains," said the Scarecrow.

"And you promised to give me a heart," said the Tin Woodman.

"And you promised to give me courage," said the Cowardly Lion.

"Is the Wicked Witch really destroyed?" asked the Voice, and Dorothy thought it trembled a little.

"Yes," she answered. "I melted her with a bucket of water."

"Dear me," said the Voice. "How sudden! Well, come to me tomorrow, for I must have time to think it over."

"You've had plenty of time already!" said the Tin Woodman angrily.

"We shan't wait a day longer," said the Scarecrow.

"You must keep your promises to us!" exclaimed Dorothy.

The Lion thought it might be as well to frighten the Wizard, so he gave a large loud roar, which was so fierce and dreadful that Toto jumped away from him in alarm and tipped over the screen that stood in a corner. As it fell with a crash they looked that way, and the next moment all of them were

> 66 Is there any child of any nationality who has not cried over the death of Bambi's mother? 99

filled with wonder. For they saw, standing in just the spot the screen had hidden, a little old man with a bald head and a wrinkled face, who seemed to be as much surprised as they were. The Tin Woodman, raising his axe, rushed towards the little man and cried out: "Who are you?"

"I am Oz, the Great and Terrible," said the little man in a trembling voice, "but don't strike me—please don't!—and I'll do anything you want me to."

Our friends looked at him in surprise and dismay.

"I thought Oz was a great Head!" said Dorothy.

"And I thought Oz was a lovely Lady!" said the Scarecrow.

"And I thought Oz was a terrible Beast!" said the Tin Woodman.

"And I thought Oz was a Ball of Fire! exclaimed the Lion.

"No, you are all wrong," said the little man meekly. "I have been making believe."

"Making believe!" cried Dorothy. "Are you not a great wizard?"

"Hush, my dear," he said. "Don't speak so loud, or you will be overheard—and I should be ruined. I'm supposed to be a great wizard."

"And aren't you?" she asked.

"Not a bit of it, my dear. I'm just a common man."

"You're more than that," said the Scarecrow in a grieved tone. "You're a humbug!"

"Exactly so!" declared the little man, rubbing his hands together as if it pleased him. "I am a humbug."

The "wizard" goes on to tell the group his story, that he was from Omaha, that he began life as a simple ventriloquist, then became a balloonist for the circus. One day his balloon got out of control and carried him far, far away from Omaha, all the way to Oz, whose people thought he was a wizard since he came to them from the skies.

"One of my greatest fears was the Witches, for while I had no magical powers at all I soon found out that the Witches were really able to do wonderful things. There were four of them in this country, and they ruled the people who live in the North and South and East and West. Fortunately the Witches of the North and South were good, and I knew they would do me no harm; but the Witches of the East and West were terribly wicked, and had they not thought I was more powerful than they themselves they would surely have destroyed me. As it was, I lived in deadly fear of them for many years; so you can imagine how pleased I was when I heard your house had fallen on the Wicked Witch of the East. When you came to me I was willing to promise anything if you would only do away with the other Witch; but, now that you have melted her, I am ashamed to say that I cannot keep my promises."

"I think you are a very bad man," said Dorothy.

"Oh no, my dear; I'm really a very good man; but I'm a very bad wizard, I must admit."

The film won several Oscars including best song for Harold Arlen and Yip Harburg. Some years later the prolific Harburg was being interviewed on television.

"Mr. Harburg, you wrote that great song, 'April in Paris'; how'd you do it? I understand you haven't even been to France!"

"Well," said the laconic lyricist, "I've never been over the rainbow either."

80 ❖ ଊ

IS THERE ANY CHILD OF ANY NATIONALITY WHO HAS NOT CRIED OVER the death of Bambi's mother?

Written by Felix Salten (1869-1945) in 1929, the timeless classic is one of the few successful attempts to humanize animals in fiction. It was made into a great full-length animated cartoon feature in 1942 by Walt Disney, and Bambi's mother's death scene was even more heart-rending than in Salten's prose version.

"Now!" said Bambi's mother, and she was off with a bound that barely skimmed the snow. Bambi rushed after her. The thunder crashed around them. Bambi saw nothing. He just kept running. The open space was crossed. Another thicket took him in. He looked around for his mother but did not see her. He kept running even though the thunder grew more distant. He stopped with a jolt when he heard another deer cry, "Is that you, Bambi?"

Bambi saw Gobo lying helplessly in the snow. "Get up, Gobo! There's not a moment to lose," cried Bambi. "Where's your mother and Faline?"

"They had to leave me here," said Gobo. "I fell down. I can't stand up. I'm too weak. Go on, Bambi." The uproar began again with new crashes of thunder coming nearer.

Suddenly young Karus pounded by. When he saw Bambi and Gobo he called to them, "Run! Don't stand there if you can run!" He was gone in a flash and his flight carried Bambi along with it. Bambi was hardly aware that he had begun to run again, and he called softly behind him, "Good-bye, Gobo."

Bambi ran until darkness closed in and the forest grew quiet. The first friend whom Bambi saw again was Ronno. "Have you seen my mother?" Bambi asked him.

"No," answered Ronno, and walked quickly away as though he did not want to discuss it further.

Late Bambi saw Faline, who explained that her mother had gone back to try to find Gobo. Bambi told how he had seen Gobo, and they grew so sad that both were crying when Aunt Ena returned.

"My poor little Gobo is gone," she cried. "I went to the place where he lay in the snow, but there was no trace of him, not even his tracks…just big tracks, His tracks. He took my Gobo."

She was silent. Then Bambi asked,

"Aunt Ena, have you seen my mother?"

"No," answered Aunt Ena gently.

Bambi never saw his mother again.

෨ ❖ ෬

ALONG WITH THE DEATH OF BAMBI'S MOTHER, ONE OF THE SADDEST reading experiences of one's childhood is a scene from Anna Sewell's *Black Beauty, The Autobiography of a Horse.* Written in 1877, the novel, like Felix Salten's *Bambi*, is a story told from the animal's point of view and is anthropomorphic. The tale ends happily for Black Beauty herself, but not for her oldest and best friend, Ginger.

One day, whilst our cab and many others were waiting outside one of the Parks, where a band was playing, a shabby old cab drove up beside ours. The horse was an old worn-out chestnut, with an ill-kept coat, and bones that showed plainly through it. The knees knuckled over, and the fore-legs were very unsteady. I had been eating some hay, and the wind rolled a little lock of it that way, and the poor creature put out her long thin neck and picked it up, and then turned and looked about for more. There was a hopeless look in the dull eye that I could not help noticing, and then, as I was thinking where I had seen that horse before, she looked full at me and said, "Black Beauty, is that you?"

It was Ginger! but how changed! The beautifully arched and glossy neck and was straight and lank, and fallen in, the clean straight legs and delicate fetlocks were swelled; the joints were grown out of shape with hard work; the face, that was once so full of spirit and life, was now full of suffering, and I could tell by the heaving of her sides, and her frequent cough, how bad her breath was.

Our drivers were standing together a little way off, so I sidled up to her a step or two, that we might have a little quiet talk. It was a sad tale that she had to tell.

After a twelvemonth's run off at Earlshall, she was considered to be fit for work again, and was sold to a gentleman. For a little while she got on very well, but after a longer gallop than usual the old strain returned, and after being rested and doctored she was again sold. In this way she changed hands several times, but always getting lower down.

"And so at last," said she, "I was bought by a man who keeps a number of cabs and horses, and lets them out. You look well off, and I am glad of it, but I could not tell you what my life has been. When they found out my weakness, they said I was not worth what they gave for me, and that I must go into one of the low cabs, and just be used up; that is what they are doing, whipping and working with never one thought of what I suffer; they paid for me, and must get it out of me, they say. The man who hires me now pays a deal of money to the owner every day, and so he has to get it back."

I was very much troubled, and I put my nose up to hers, but I could say nothing to comfort her. I think she was pleased to see me, for she said, "You are the only friend I ever had."

Just then her driver came up, and with a yank at her mouth backed her out of the line and drove off, leaving me very sad indeed.

A short time after this a cart with a dead horse in it passed our cab-stand. The head hung out of the cart-tail, the lifeless tongue was slowly dropping with blood, and the sunken eyes! But I can't speak of them, the sight was too dreadful. It was a chestnut horse with a long thin neck. I saw a white streak down the forehead. I believe it was Ginger; I hoped it was, for then her troubles would be over. Oh! If men were more merciful, they would shoot us before we came to such misery.

The story, which has been made into several films, was a huge success when it was published and apparently was instrumental in bringing about reforms in the way cab horses in Victorian England were treated and cared for.

13

Endings

———

Longfellow said, "Great is the art of the beginning, but greater the art of ending."

I would tell a fledgling writer that the ending scene of a story was as important as the beginning, except for the fact that if the beginning isn't well written and intriguing, the reader will never get to the ending.

Having said that, let us look at three excellent ending scenes of novels by Ernest Hemingway. They are brief and exactly right for the stories that have preceded them.

At the end of *The Sun Also Rises*, the highly-sexed Lady Brett and the hero Jake Barnes, who has been rendered impotent by a war wound, face a bleak if non-existent future. Together, in a taxi in Madrid, Brett maintains that they could have had a life together.

> "Oh, Jake," Brett said, "we could have had such a damned good time together."
>
> Ahead was a mounted policeman in khaki directing traffic. He raised his baton. The taxi slowed, suddenly pressing Brett against me.
>
> "Yes," I said. "Isn't it pretty to think so."

Hemingway's novel *For Whom the Bell Tolls* begins with this scene:

> He lay flat on the brown, pine-needled floor of the forest, his chin on his folded arms, and high overhead the wind blew in the tops of the pine trees.

Four hundred seventy pages later, the book ends with Robert Jordan again lying on pine needles. Now his hip is broken, his submachine gun at the ready, and he is awaiting certain death:

> Lieutenant Berrendo, watching the trail, came riding up, his thin face serious and grave. His submachine gun lay across his saddle in the crook of his left arm. Robert Jordan lay behind the tree, holding onto himself very carefully and delicately to keep his hands steady. He was waiting until the officer reached the sunlit place where the first trees of the pine forest joined the green slope of the meadow. He could feel his heart beating against the pine needle floor of the forest.

The end.

We do not need to see the actual death of Robert Jordan. It is a perfect scene for this novel. Again,

—less is more.

In a like manner, Hemingway's simply-written end to *A Farewell to Arms* is all the more powerful for being so understated and reserved.

Lieutenant Henry learns that his great love, Catherine, has died. The doctor speaks to the shattered young soldier in the hospital:

> "Good-night," he said. "I cannot take you to your hotel?"
>
> "No, thank you."
>
> "It was the only thing to do," he said. "The operation proved—"
>
> "I do not want to talk about it," I said.
>
> "I would like to take you to your hotel."
>
> "No, thank you."
>
> He went down the hall. I went to the door of the room.
>
> "You can't come in now," one of the nurses said.
>
> "Yes I can," I said.
>
> "You can't come in yet."
>
> "You get out," I said. "The other one too."
>
> But after I had got them out and shut the door and turned off the light it wasn't any good. It was like saying good-by to a

statue. After a while I went out and left the hospital and walked back to the hotel in the rain.

It is said that the author wrote thirty-three endings for the novel, finally finding the perfect one. When we read some of the rejected ones, we can believe even more fervently in the maxim:

"Stories aren't written—they are rewritten."

One of the rejected endings was this:

> That is all there is to the story. Catherine died and you will die and I will die and that is all I can promise you.

In another, he made little sense:

> See Naples and die is a fine idea: You will live to hate its guts if you live there. Perhaps there is no luck in a Peninsula.

Sometimes he waxed grandiose:

> That is all there is to this story. There is supposed to be something which controls all these things and not one sparrow is forgotten before God.

One ending sounded as though he had entered a Bad Hemingway contest and won:

> After people die you have to bury them but you do not have to write about it. You do not have to write about an undertaker. Nor the business of burial in a foreign country. Nor do you have to write about that day and the next night nor the day after nor the night after nor all the days after and all the nights after while numbness turns to snow and snow blunts with use. In writing you have a certain choice that you do not have in life.

๛ ❖ ☙

THERE ARE CERTAIN SHORT STORIES THAT EVERY WOULD-BE WRITER ought to read; one of the classics, written by Guy De Maupassant (1850-1893), is "The Necklace."

The story begins:

> She was one of those lovely and charming young ladies, born as though by an error of fate into a family of clerks. She had no dowry, no hopes, and no means of becoming known, appreciated, loved and married by a man either rich or distinguished, so she allowed herself to marry a minor clerk in the Board of Education.

He adores her, but they are poor and she is very unhappy with her lot. When they are unexpectedly invited to a grand governmental ball, she complains that she can't go because she hasn't a proper dress. The husband takes the money he was going to use to buy a shotgun for hunting and buys her a fancy gown. But, she complains, she can't go because all the rich women will have jewels and she will have none. "Why not borrow one from that rich friend from your childhood?" he suggests.

Matilda goes to the wealthy Madam Forestier who is pleased to lend her a fabulous-looking diamond necklace. Matilda has a fine time at the party, but upon arriving back at their modest home she finds to her horror that the necklace has been lost.

By borrowing from everyone he knows, the husband manages to scrape up enough money, an astronomical sum, to buy a necklace which closely resembles the lost one; she returns it to an unsuspecting Madame Forestier. Then husband and wife set about trying to repay the huge debt. Here's how the story ends:

> Mme Loisel now knew the horrible life of necessity. She did her part, however, completely, heroically. It was necessary to pay this frightful debt. She would pay it. They sent away the maid; they changed their lodgings; they rented some rooms under a mansard roof.
>
> She learned the heavy cares of a household, the odious work of a kitchen. She washed the dishes, using her rosy nails upon the greasy pots and the bottoms of the stewpans. She washed the soiled linen, the chemises and dishcloths, which she

hung on the line to dry; she took down the refuse to the street each morning and brought up the water, stopping at each landing to breathe. And, clothed like a woman of the people, she went to the grocer's, the butcher's and the fruiterer's with her basket on her arm, shopping, haggling to the last sou her miserable money.

Every month it was necessary to renew some notes, thus obtaining time, and to pay others.

The husband worked evenings, putting the books of some merchants in order, and nights he often did copying at five sous a page.

And this life lasted for ten years.

At the end of ten years they had restored all, all, with interest of the usurer, and accumulated interest, besides.

Mme Loisel seemed old now. She had become a strong, hard woman, the poor woman of the poor household. Her hair badly dressed, her skirts awry, her hands red, she spoke in a loud tone and washed the floors in large pails of water. But sometimes, when her husband was at the office, she would seat herself before the window and think of that evening party of former times, of that ball where she was so beautiful and so flattered.

How would it have been if she had not lost that necklace? Who knows? Who knows? How singular is life and how full of changes! How small a thing will ruin or save one!

One Sunday, as she was taking a walk in the Champs-Elysées to rid herself of the cares of the week, she suddenly perceived a woman walking with a child. It was Mme Forestier, still young, still pretty, still attractive. Mme Loisel was affected. Should she speak to her? Yes, certainly. And now that she had paid, she would tell her all. Why not?

She approached her. "Good morning, Jeanne."

Her friend did not recognize her and was astonished to be so familiarly addressed by this common personage. She stammered:

"But, madame—I do not know—You must be mistaken."

"No, I am Matilda Loisel."

Her friend uttered a cry of astonishment: "Oh! My poor Matilda! How you have changed."

"Yes, I have had some hard days since I saw you, and some miserable ones—and all because of you."

"Because of me? How is that?"

"You recall the diamond necklace that you loaned me to wear to the minister's ball?"

"Yes, very well."

"Well, I lost it."

"How is that, since you returned it to me?"

"I returned another to you exactly like it. And it has taken us ten years to pay for it. You can understand that it was not easy for us who have nothing. But it is over, and I am satisfied."

Mme Forestier stopped short. She said:

"You say that you bought a diamond necklace to replace mine?"

"Yes. You did not perceive it then? They were just alike."

And she smiled with a proud and simple joy. Mme Forestier was touched and took both her hands as she replied:

"Oh, my poor Matilda! Mine were false. They were not worth over five hundred francs!"

And we never learn what happens to the hapless couple.

ℰ ❖ ℛ

ANTON CHEKHOV ONCE DECLARED: "MY OWN EXPERIENCE IS THAT once a story has been written, one has to cross out the beginning and the end. It is there that we authors do most of our lying."

There is no lying in the last lovely scene of *Our Town*, perhaps America's most popular play. Written by Thornton Wilder in 1938, it still remains a mainstay for summer theaters around the country. Set in a small New Hampshire village around the beginning of the last century, it tells the simple love story of George Gibbs and Emily Webb, and it does so with the help of The Stage Manager, an omniscient presence who remains informally on the stage and explains much of the action.

Nine years after their marriage, Emily dies in childbirth. In the final poignant scene, the dead come briefly to life, and Emily relives her twelfth birthday party and exchanges views with others from the graveyard.

MR. WEBB (*Off stage*): Where's my girl? Where's my birth-day girl?

EMILY (*In a loud voice to the stage manager*): I can't. I can't go on. It goes so fast. We don't have time to look at one another.

She breaks down sobbing.

The lights dim on the left half of the stage.

MRS. WEBB disappears.

I didn't realize. So all that was going on and we never noticed. Take me back—up the hill—to my grave. But first: Wait! One more look. Good-by, Good-by, world. Good-by, Grover's Corners…Mama and Papa. Good-by to clocks ticking…and Mama's sunflowers. And food and coffee. And new-ironed dresses and hot baths…and sleeping and waking up. Oh, earth, you're too wonderful for anybody to realize you.

She looks toward the stage manager and asks abruptly, through her tears:

Do any human beings ever realize life while they live it?—every, every minute?

STAGE MANAGER: No. (*Pause*) The saints and poets, maybe—they do some.

EMILY: I'm ready to go back. *She returns to her chair beside Mrs. Gibbs. Pause.*

MRS. GIBBS: Were you happy?

EMILY: No…I should have listened to you. That's all human beings are! Just blind people.

MRS. GIBBS: Look, it's clearing up. The stars are coming out.

EMILY: Oh, Mr. Stimson, I should have listened to them.

SIMON STIMSON (*With mounting violence; bitingly*): Yes, now you know. Now you know! That's what it was to be alive. To move about in a cloud of ignorance; to go up and down trampling on the feelings of those…of those about you. To spend and waste time as though you had a million years. To be always at the mercy of one self-centered passion, or another. Now you know—that's the happy existence you wanted to go back to. Ignorance and blindness.

MRS. GIBBS (*Spiritedly*): Simon Stimson, that ain't the whole truth and you know it. Emily, look at that star. I forget its name.

A MAN AMONG THE DEAD: My boy Joel was a sailor,— knew 'em all. He'd set on the porch evenings and tell 'em all by name. Yes, sir, wonderful!

ANOTHER MAN AMONG THE DEAD: A star's mighty good company.

A WOMAN AMONG THE DEAD: Yes. Yes, 'tis.

SIMON STIMSON: Here's one of *them* coming.

THE DEAD: That's funny. 'Tain't no time for one of them to be here.—Goodness sakes.

EMILY: Mother Gibbs, it's George.

MRS. GIBBS: Sh, dear. Just rest yourself.

EMILY: It's George.

GEORGE enters from the left, and slowly comes toward them.

A MAN FROM AMONG THE DEAD: And my boy, Joel, who knew the stars—he used to say it took millions of years for that speck o'light to git to the earth. Don't seem like a body could believe it, but that's what he used to say—millions of years.

GEORGE sinks to his knees then falls full length at Emily's feet.

A WOMAN AMONG THE DEAD: Goodness! That ain't no way to behave!

MRS. SOAMES: He ought to be home.

EMILY: Mother Gibbs?

MRS. GIBBS: Yes, Emily?

EMILY: They don't understand, do they?

MRS. GIBBS: No, dear. They don't understand.

The STAGE MANAGER appears at the right, one hand on a dark curtain which he slowly draws across the scene. In the distance a clock is heard striking the hour very faintly.

STAGE MANAGER: Most everybody's asleep in Grover's Corners. There are a few lights on: Shorty Hawkins, down at the depot, has just watched the Albany train go by. And at the livery stable somebody's setting up late and talking.—Yes, it's clearing up. There are the stars—doing their old, old crisscross journeys in the sky. Scholars haven't settled the matter yet, but they seem to think there are no living beings up there. Just chalk...or fire. Only this one is straining away, straining away all the time to make something of itself. The strain's so bad that every sixteen hours everybody lies down and gets a rest. *(He winds his watch.)* Hm…Eleven o'clock in Grover's Corners.—You get a good rest, too. Good night.

THE END

Talk about "aiming for the heart"!

Our Town was made into a fine film in 1940, and Martha Scott, a first-time actress on Broadway, repeated the role of Emily on the screen and was nominated for an Oscar.

ಜಾ ❖ ಚಿ

ANY WOULD-BE WRITER FACED IN HIS STORY WITH THE DEATH OF a character would do well to study how Emma Bovary's death is handled. Surely the longest and most graphic death scene in all literature comes at the end of *Madame Bovary*. The eponymous protagonist of Flaubert's 1857 masterpiece, disillusioned by her lovers, bored with her nice husband, and swamped with debts, swallows a cup of arsenic.

> "Ah, it's nothing very much—dying!" she thought. "I shall just drop off to sleep, and it will all be over."

But not at all. The author, the son of a doctor, knew a lot about medicine and the effects of arsenic. In page after page he spares us nothing, the thirst, "the horrible taste of ink," the vomiting, the "icy coldness creeping up from her feet to her heart," the shuddering convulsions. Then there is a moment of calm, and the poor husband takes heart.

> "Perhaps, after all, we ought not to despair," thought he.
> And indeed she looked all round about her, slowly, like one waking from a dream; then, in quite a strong voice, she asked for her mirror, and remained looking into it for some time, until great tears began to trickle from her eyes. Then she sighed, turned away her head, and sank down again on the pillow.
> And immediately her breathing became very rapid. The

full length of her tongue protruded from her mouth. Her wandering eyes began to grow pale, like a pair of lamp globes in which the light was waning, so that you would have thought her already dead, but for the terrible heaving of her sides, shaken by some raging tempest, as though the soul were leaping and straining to be free. Félicité knelt down before the crucifix, and even the apothecary bent his hams a little, while Monsieur Canivet stood gazing out vaguely on to the Square. Bournisien had begun to pray again, his face bowed down upon the edge of the bed, his long black soutane training out behind him across the floor. Charles was on the other side, on his knees, his arms outstretched towards Emma. He had taken her hands, and was pressing them in his, trembling at her every heart-beat, as a man might start at the sound of a collapsing ruin. As the death-rattle grew more insistent, the priest redoubled the speed of his orisons; they mingled with Bovary's choking sobs, and sometimes all seemed drowned in the low murmur of the Latin syllables, which sounded like the tinkling of a passing bell.

Suddenly there was a noise of heavy clogs on the pavement outside and the scraping of a stick, and a voice, a raucous voice, began to sing,

> *Now skies are bright, the summer's here,*
> *A maiden thinks upon her dear.*

Emma sat bolt upright like a corpse suddenly galvanized into life, her hair disheveled, her eyes fixed in a glassy stare, gaping with horror.

> *And to gather up with care*
> *What the weary reaper leaves,*
> *My Nanette goes gleaning there,*
> *Down among the golden sheaves.*

"The blind man!" she cried, and broke out into a laugh—a ghastly, frantic, despairing laugh—thinking she saw the hideous features of the wretched being, rising up to strike terror to her soul, on the very threshold of eternal night.

She stooped low, the wind blew high,
What a sight for mortal eye!

She fell back in a paroxysm on to the mattress. They hurried to her side. Emma was no more.

 ∽ ❖ ⁊

THE MILLIONS OF HAPPY FANS OF *MY FAIR LADY*, ONE OF THE MOST popular musicals of all time, would be disappointed and disillusioned to be exposed to the ending of the genesis of that work, George Bernard Shaw's *Pygmalion*. So sparkling and "modern," it is hard to believe that it was written in 1912. While the play has many of the same scenes and lines of the musical and the film, it has an edgier feel to it, and Professor Higgins is even more curmudgeonly than Rex Harrison. For example, here is the scene after the garden party (the Grand Ball in the musical), and Higgins has won his bet that he could pass Liza off as a duchess by her speech alone.

> *She sits down in Higgins's chair and holds on hard to the arms. Finally she gives way and flings herself furiously on the floor, raging.*

HIGGINS *(in despairing wrath outside)*: What the devil have I done with my slippers? *(He appears at the door.)*

LIZA *(snatching up the slippers, and hurling them at him one after the other with all her force)*: There are your slippers. And there. Take your slippers; and may you never have a day's luck with them!

HIGGINS *(astounded)*: What on earth—! *(He comes to her.)* What's the matter? Get up. *(He pulls her up.)* Anything wrong?

LIZA *(breathless)*: Nothing wrong—with you. I've won your bet for you, haven't I? That's enough for you. *I* don't matter, I suppose.

HIGGINS: You won my bet! You! Presumptuous insect! *I* won it. What did you throw those slippers at me for?

LIZA: Because I wanted to smash your face. I'd like to kill you, you selfish brute. Why didn't you leave me where you picked me out of—in the gutter? You thank God it's all over, and that now you can throw me back again there, do you *(She crisps her fingers frantically.)*

HIGGINS *(looking at her in cool wonder)*: The creature is nervous, after all.

LIZA *(gives a suffocated scream of fury, and instinctively darts her nails at his face)*!!

HIGGINS *(catching her wrists)*: Ah! Would you? Claws in, you cat. How dare you show your temper to me? Sit down and be quiet. *(He throws her roughly into the easy-chair.)*

LIZA *(crushed by superior strength and weight)*: What's to become of me? What's to become of me?

HIGGINS: How the devil do I know what's to become of you? What does it matter what becomes of you?

LIZA: You don't care. I know you don't care. You wouldn't care if I was dead. I'm nothing to you—not so much as them slippers.

HIGGINS *(thundering)*: Those slippers.

LIZA *(with bitter submission)*: Those slippers. I didn't think it made any difference now.

A pause. Eliza hopeless and crushed. Higgins a little uneasy.

HIGGINS *(in his loftiest manner)*: Why have you begun going on like this? May I ask whether you complain of your treatment here?

LIZA: No.

HIGGINS: Has anybody behaved badly to you? Colonel Pickering? Mrs. Pearce? Any of the servants?

LIZA: No.

HIGGINS: I presume you don't pretend that *I* have treated you badly?

LIZA: No.

HIGGINS. I am glad to hear it. *(He moderates his tone.)* Perhaps you're tired after the strain of the day. Will you have a glass of champagne? *(He moves towards the door.)*

LIZA: No. *(Recollecting her manners)* Thank you.

HIGGINS *(good-humored again)*: This has been coming on you for some days. I suppose it was natural for you to be anxious about the garden party. But that's all over now. *(He pats her kindly on the shoulder. She writhes.)* There's nothing more to worry about.

LIZA: No. Nothing more for you to worry about. *(She suddenly rises and gets away from him by going to the piano bench, where she sits and hides her face.)* Oh God! I wish I was dead.

HIGGINS *(staring after her in sincere surprise)*: Why? In heaven's name, why? *(Reasonably, going to her)* Listen to me, Eliza. All this irritation is purely subjective.

LIZA: I don't understand. I'm too ignorant.

HIGGINS: It's only imagination. Low spirits and nothing else.

Quite a contrast from the joyous celebration after the triumphant success as portrayed in the musical and film (Julie Andrews on the stage, Audrey Hepburn in the 1964 film).

And as for the outcome! Shaw shrank from sentimentality and cliché, and he was not about to let the playgoer leave his play with a happy feeling. Liza says: "Then I shall not see you again, Professor. Goodbye."

Higgins arrogantly orders her to buy him some gloves, a tie, et cetera, and she retorts disdainfully, "Buy them yourself," and sweeps out.

But Higgins says, sunnily, "She'll buy 'em all right enough." The End.

But does she?

In an afterword, Shaw volunteers, to the horror of us incurable romantics:

> This being the state of human affairs, what is Eliza fairly sure to do when she is placed between Freddy [a handsome, yet docile, aristocrat who falls in love with Eliza] and Higgins? Will she look forward to a lifetime of fetching Higgins's slippers or to a lifetime of Freddy fetching hers? There can be no doubt about the answer. Unless Freddy is biologically repulsive to her, and Higgins biologically attractive to a degree that overwhelms all her other instincts, she will, if she marries either of them, marry Freddy.
>
> And that is just what Eliza did.

80 ❖ CR

PERHAPS THE LOUDEST SLAM OF ANY STAGE DOOR IN ANY STAGE PLAY in any language in history comes in the scene at the end of Henrik Ibsen's cataclysmic 1879 play, *A Doll's House*. The noise reverberated around the world, above all with those championing women's rights, and it still ends the play on a powerful note, a plea for the rights of all individuals throughout the world.

At the end of the play, Nora, after a complicated plot, sees for the first time what her husband, Torvald, is—a selfish, pretentious, hypocrite. She has made the decision to leave him and her children in this famous scene:

> NORA: As I am now, I am no wife for you.
>
> HELMER: I have it in me to become a different man.
>
> NORA: Perhaps—if your doll is taken away from you.
>
> HELMER: But to part!—to part from you! No, no, Nora, I can't entertain that idea.
>
> NORA *(going out to the right)*: That makes it all the more certain that it must be done.
>
> *She comes back with her cloak and hat and a small bag which she puts on a chair by the table.*
>
> HELMER: Nora, Nora, not now! Wait till to-morrow.
>
> NORA *(putting on her cloak):* I cannot spend the night in a strange man's room.
> HELMER: But can't we live here like brother and sister—?
>
> NORA *(putting on her hat)*: You know very well that would not last long. *(Puts the shawl round her.)* Good-bye, Torvald. I won't see the little ones. I know they are in better hands than mine. As I am now, I can be of no use to them.
>
> HELMER: But some day, Nora—some day?
>
> NORA: How can I tell? I have no idea what is going to become of me.
>
> HELMER: But you are my wife, whatever becomes of you.
>
> NORA: Listen, Torvald. I have heard that when a wife deserts her husband's house, as I am doing now, he is legally freed

from all obligations towards her. In any case I set you free from all your obligations. You are not to feel yourself bound in the slightest way, any more than I shall. There must be perfect freedom on both sides. See here is your ring back. Give me mine.

HELMER: That too?

NORA: That too.

HELMER: Here it is.

NORA: That's right. Now it is all over. I have put the keys here. The maids know all about everything in the house—better than I do. To-morrow, after I have left her, Christine will come here and pack up my own things that I brought with me from home. I will have them sent after me.

HELMER: All over! All over!—Nora, shall you never think of me again?

NORA: I know I shall often think of you and the children and this house.

HELMER: May I write to you, Nora?

NORA: No—never. You must not do that.

HELMER: But at least let me send you—

NORA: Nothing—nothing—

HELMER: Let me help you if you are in want.

NORA: No. I can receive nothing from a stranger.

HELMER: Nora—can I never be anything more than a stranger to you?

NORA *(taking her bag)*: Ah, Torvald, the most wonderful thing of all would have to happen.

HELMER: Tell me what that would be!

NORA: Both you and I would have to be so changed that—. Oh, Torvald, I don't believe any longer in wonderful things happening.

HELMER: But I will believe in it. Tell me? So changed that—?

NORA: That our life together would be a real wedlock. Good-bye.

(She goes out through the hall.)

HELMER *(sinks down on a chair at the door and buries his face in his hands)*: Nora! Nora! *(Looks round, and rises.)* Empty. She is gone. *(A hope flashes across his mind.)* The most wonderful thing of all—? *(The sound of a door shutting is heard from below. A loud LOUD door shutting.)*

෯ ❖ ଔ

WHAT OTHER NOVEL CAN BOAST THE MOST FAMOUS OPENING SENTENCE as well as the equally famous last sentence?

Charles Dickens begins *A Tale of Two Cities* with a very long sentence which begins: "It was the best of times, it was the worst of times..." (which brings to mind the *New Yorker* magazine's cartoon of a publisher telling the hapless author: "Now, Mr. Dickens, it was either the best of times or the worst, you can't have it both ways.")

The last two sentences of the novel, though so frequently quoted, are not exactly said by the protagonist as most people think.

Sydney Carton, a dissolute young Englishman, redeems himself at the end of the novel by bribing his way into prison in order to take the place of his great friend, Charles Darnay, at the guillotine. Here is the beginning of the novel's conclusion:

They said of him, about the city that night, that it was the peacefullest man's face ever beheld there. Many added that he looked sublime and prophetic.

One of the most remarkable sufferers by the same axe—a woman—had asked at the foot of the same scaffold, not long before, to be allowed to write down the thoughts that were inspiring her. If he had given an utterance to his, and they were prophetic, they would have been these:

"I see Barsad, and Cly, Defarge, The Vengeance, the Juryman, the Judge, long ranks of the new oppressors who have risen on the destruction of the old, perishing by this retributive instrument, before it shall cease out of its present use. I see a beautiful city and a brilliant people rising from this abyss, and, in their struggles to be truly free, in their triumphs and defeats, through long long years to come, I see the evil of this time and of the previous time of which this is the natural birth, gradually making expiation for itself and wearing out.

It is the author conjecturing about what might have been Carton's thoughts and finally ends with these words:

"I see that child who lay upon her bosom and who bore my name, a man winning his way up in that path of life which once was mine. I see him winning it so well, that my name is made illustrious there by the light of his. I see the blots I threw upon it, faded away. I see him, foremost of just judges and honoured men, bringing a boy of my name, with a forehead that I know and golden hair, to this place—then fair to look upon, with not a trace of this day's disfigurement—and I hear him tell the child my story, with a tender and a faltering voice.

"It is a far, far better thing that I do, than I have ever done; it is a far, far better rest that I go to than I have ever known."

So, contrary to what most people think, the familiar words "It is a far, far better thing that I do"—spoken by Ronald Colman at the end of the great 1935 MGM film—emanate not exactly from Sydney Carton but from his creator, Charles Dickens.

❧ ❖ ❦

FEW, IF ANY, MODERN PLAYS HAVE HAD THE GUT-WRENCHING THIRD act scene of William Gibson's play *The Miracle Worker*. Anyone who saw the first 1957 version on television's distinguished Playhouse 90 series, the subsequent Broadway play, and then the 1962 splendid film, can never forget that one great final scene before the curtain. Everyone knows it is based on an actual situation: Slum-raised Annie Sullivan, half-blind herself, is hired to "teach" blind-deaf-mute six-and-a-half year old Helen Keller. At this point, Helen is a raging hellion, whom the parents, the Kellers, insist on coddling and indulging, contrary to Annie's tough-love ideas of how to deal with the terrible problem of the girl's total lack of communication.

Kate, Helen's mother, and Aunt Ev and Uncle James are in this final scene, as is Keller, the father. Helen has had a tantrum at the table and thrown a pitcher of water at Annie.

> *Annie has pulled Helen downstairs again by one hand,*
> *the pitcher in her other hand, down the porch steps, and*
> *across the yard to the pump. She puts Helen's hand on the*
> *pump handle, grimly.*

ANNIE: All right. Pump.

> *Helen touches her cheek, waits uncertain.*

No, she's not here. Pump!

> *She forces Helen's hand to work the handle, then lets go.*
> *And Helen obeys. She pumps till the water comes, then*
> *Annie puts the pitcher in her other hand and guides it*
> *under the spout, and the water tumbling half into and*
> *half around the pitcher douses Helen's hand. Annie takes*
> *over the handle to keep water coming, and does auto-*
> *matically what she has done so many times before, spells*
> *into Helen's free palm:*

Water. W, a, t, e, r. *Water.* It has a—*name*—

*And by now the miracle happens. Helen drops the pitcher
on the slab under the spout, it shatters. She stands trans-
fixed. Annie freezes on the pump handle: there is a change
in the sundown light, and with it a change in Helen's face,
some light coming into it we have never seen there, some
struggle in the depths behind it; and her lips tremble, trying to remember something the muscles around them once
knew, till at last it finds its way out, painfully, a baby
sound buried under the debris of years of dumbness.*

HELEN: Wah. Wah.

(And again, with great effort)

*Helen plunges her hand into the dwindling water, spells
into her own palm. Then she gropes frantically, Annie
reaches for her hand, and Helen spells into Annie's hand.*

ANNIE [whispering]: Yes.

Helen spells into it again.

Yes!

*Helen grabs at the handle, pumps for more water, plunges
her hand into its spurt and grabs Annie's to spell it again.*

Yes! Oh, my dear—

*She falls to her knees to clasp Helen's hand, but Helen
pulls it free, stands almost bewildered, then drops to the
ground, pats it swiftly, holds up her palm, imperious. Annie
spells into it:*

Ground

Helen spells it back.

Yes!

> *Helen whirls to the pump, pats it, holds up her palm, and Annie spells into it:*

Pump.

> *Helen spells it back.*

Yes! Yes!

> *Now Helen is in such an excitement she is possessed, wild, trembling, cannot be still, turns, runs, falls on the porch steps, claps it, reaches out her palm, and Annie is at it instantly to spell:*

Step.

> *Helen has no time to spell back now, she whirls groping, to touch anything, encounters the trellis, shakes it, thrusts out her palm, and Annie while spelling to her cries wildly at the house.*

Trellis. Mrs. Keller! *Mrs. Keller!*

> *Inside, Kate starts to her feet. Helen scrambles back onto the porch, groping, and finds the bell string, tugs it; the bell rings, the distant chimes begin tolling the hour, all the bells in town seem to break into speech while Helen reaches out and Annie spells feverishly into her hand. Kate hurries out, with Keller after her; Aunt Ev is on her feet, to peer out the window; only James remains at the table, and with a napkin wipes his damp brow. From up right and left the servants—Viney, the two Negro children, the other servant—run in, and stand watching from a distance as Helen, ringing the bell, with her other hand encounters her mother's skirt; when she throws a hand out, Annie spells into it:*

Mother.

Keller now seizes Helen's hand, she touches him, gestures a hand, and Annie again spells:

Papa—She *knows!*

Kate and Keller go to their knees, stammering, clutching Helen to them, and Annie steps unsteadily back to watch the threesome, Helen spelling wildly into Kate's hand, then into Keller's, Kate spelling back into Helen's; they cannot keep their hands off her, and rock her in their clasp. Then Helen gropes, feels nothing, turns all around, pulls free, and comes with both hands groping, to find Annie. She encounters Annie's thighs, Annie kneels to her, Helen's hand pats Annie's cheek impatiently, points a finger, and waits; and Annie spells into it:

Teacher.

Helen spells it back, slowly; Annie nods.

Teacher.

She holds Helen's hand to her cheek. Presently Helen withdraws it, not jerkily, only with reserve, and retreats a step. She stands thinking it over, then turns again and stumbles back to her parents. They try to embrace her, but she has something else in mind, it is to get the keys, and she hits Kate's pocket until Kate digs them out for her.

Annie with her own load of emotion has retreated, her back turned, toward the pump, to sit; Kate moves to Helen, touches her hand questioningly, and Helen spells a word to her. Kate comprehends it, their first act of verbal communication, and she can hardly utter the word aloud, in wonder, gratitude, and deprivation; it is a moment in which she simultaneously finds and loses a child.

KATE: Teacher?

Annie turns; and Kate, facing Helen in her direction by the shoulders, holds her back, holds her back, and then relinquishes her. Helen feels her way across the yard, rather shyly, and when her moving hands touch Annie's skirts she stops. Then she holds out the keys and places them in Annie's hand. For a moment neither of them moves. Then Helen slides into Annie's arms, and lifting away her smoked glasses, kisses her on the cheek. Annie gathers her in.

Kate torn both ways turns from this, gestures the servants off, and makes her way into the house, on Keller's arm. The servants go, in separate directions.

The lights are half down now, except over the pump. Annie and Helen are here, alone in the yard. Annie has found Helen's hand, almost without knowing it, and she spells slowly into it, her voice unsteady, whispering:)

ANNIE: I, love, Helen.

She clutches the child to her, tight this time, not spelling, whispering into her hair.

Forever, and—

She stops. The lights over the pump are taking on the color of the past, and it brings Annie's head up, her eyes opening, in fear; and as slowly as though drawn she rises, to listen, with her hand on Helen's shoulders. She waits, waits, listening with ears and eyes both, slowly here, slowly there: and hears only silence. There are no voices. The color passes on, and when her eyes come back to Helen she can breathe the end of her phrase without fear:

—ever.

In the family room Kate has stood over the table, staring at Helen's plate, with Keller at her shoulder; now James takes a step to move her chair in, and Kate sits, with head erect, and Keller inclines his head to James; so it is Aunt Ev, hesitant, and rather humble, who moves to the door.

Outside Helen tugs at Annie's hand, and Annie comes in with it. Helen pulls her toward the house; and hand in hand, they cross the yard, and ascend the porch steps, in the rising lights, to where Aunt Ev is holding the door open for them.

The curtain ends the play.

Whew. Once again, aim for the heart.

And then one thinks of all the incredible things that Helen Keller went on, in her incredible real life, to accomplish, never hearing, or seeing—and one mists up.

A unique situation in theatrical history comes out of this great play:

In the original Broadway play of *The Miracle Worker*, Anne Bancroft played Annie Sullivan and Patty Duke played the child. In the film version, 1962, directed by Arthur Penn, they repeated the roles and both won Oscars; in 1979, in a television version, Duke played the role of the mentor!

℘ ❖ ℞

THE NOVEL *THE GRAPES OF WRATH*, BY JOHN STEINBECK, HAS been both glorified and vilified since its publication in 1939.

It has also been parodied in many ways; for example, in the fifties there was a distinguished but disgruntled supervisor in San Francisco named Bill Roth who constantly railed against the Establishment's actions, no matter what they might be. So, of course, the celebrated *Chronicle* columnist, Herb Caen, headlined many of his columns: "The Gripes of Roth."

The novel was an enormous and controversial blockbuster. It is still powerful, as is the film which was made in 1940. Directed by John Ford and starring Henry Fonda, the Nunnally Johnson screenplay followed the novel's scenes closely, including the moving, and highly unusual, final one. (Both Fonda and Jane Darwell as Tom and Ma Joad, poor immigrants from Oklahoma on their trek to California, received Oscars.)

In the last scene of the book, the Joad family make it out of a rainstorm to a stranger's barn. Ma Joad's daughter, Rose of Sharon, has very recently given birth to a stillborn child, and is still weak.

Winfield said, "Ma!" and the rain roaring on the roof drowned his voice. "*Ma!*"

"What is it? What you want?"

"Look! In the corner."

Ma looked. There were two figures in the gloom; a man who lay on his back, and a boy sitting beside him, his eyes wide, staring at the newcomers. As she looked, the boy got slowly up to his feet and came toward her. His voice croaked. "You own this here?"

"No," Ma said. "Jus' come in outa the wet. We got a sick girl. You got a dry blanket we could use an' get her wet clothes off?"

The boy went back to the corner and brought a dirty comfort and held it out to Ma.

"Thank ya," she said. "What's the matter'th that fella?"

The boy spoke in a croaking monotone. "Fust he was sick—but now he's starvin'."

"What?"

"Starvin'. Got sick in the cotton. He ain't et for six days."

Ma walked to the corner and looked down at the man. He was about fifty, his whiskery face gaunt, and his open eyes were vague and staring. The boy stood beside her. "Your pa?" Ma asked.

"Yeah! Says he wasn' hungry, or he jus' et. Give me the food. Now he's too weak. Can't hardly move."

The pounding of the rain decreased to a soothing swish on the roof. The gaunt man moved his lips. Ma knelt beside him and put her ear close. His lips moved again.

"Sure," Ma said. "You jus' be easy. He'll be awright. You jus' wait'll I get them wet clo'es off'n my girl."

Ma went back to the girl. "Now slip 'em off," she said.

She held the comfort up to screen her from view. And when she was naked, Ma folded the comfort about her.

The boy was at her side again explaining, "I didn' know. He said he et, or he wasn' hungry. Las' night I went an' bust a winda an' stoled some bread. Made 'im chew 'er down. But he puked it all up, an' then he was weaker. Got to have soup or milk. You folks got money to git milk?"

Ma said, "Hush. Don' worry. We'll figger somepin out."

Suddenly the boy cried, "He's dyin', I tell you! He's starvin' to death, I tell you."

"Hush," said Ma. She looked at Pa and Uncle John standing helplessly gazing at the sick man. She looked at Rose of Sharon huddled in the comfort. Ma's eyes passed Rose of Sharon's eyes, and then came back to them. And the two women looked deep into each other. The girl's breath came short and gasping.

She said, "Yes."

Ma smiled. "I knowed you would. I knowed!" She looked down at her hands, tight-locked in her lap.

Rose of Sharon whispered, "Will—will you all—go out?" The rain whisked lightly on the roof.

Ma leaned forward and with her palm she brushed the tousled hair back from her daughter's forehead, and she kissed her on the forehead. Ma got up quickly. "Come on, you fellas," she called. "You come out in the tool shed."

Ruthie opened her mouth to speak. "Hush," Ma said. "Hush and git." She herded them through the door, drew the boy with her; and she closed the squeaking door.

For a minute Rose of Sharon sat still in the whispering barn. Then she hoisted her tired body up and drew the comfort about her. She moved slowly to the corner and stood looking down at the wasted face, into the wide, frightened eyes. Then slowly she lay down beside him. He shook his head slowly from side to side. Rose of Sharon loosened one side of the blanket and bared her breast. "You got to," she said. She squirmed closer and pulled his head close. "There!" she said. "There." Her hand moved behind his head and supported it. Her fingers moved gently in his hair. She looked up and across the barn, and her lips came together and smiled mysteriously.

Unbelievably, several influential groups protested the book as being obscene because of this last scene.

ဢ ❖ ᘒ

WILLIAM BOTIBOL IS THE WIMPY PROTAGONIST OF ROALD DAHL'S memorable *tour de force* short story, "Dip in the Pool," which appeared in the *New Yorker* magazine in 1952 and became a word-of-mouth sensation. The last scene is hard to forget.

Botibol is on a fancy transatlantic liner, but he is virtually broke. When he learns that betting on the ship's mileage could net him some seven thousand dollars, he decides to bet every cent he owns, six hundred dollars, on a ticket in the passengers' pool. The ship has been struggling through a storm for three days, so Botibol has bet on very low mileage. But the next day, the day the winner will be announced, the weather clears dramatically, the seas are calm, and the ship starts to pick up mileage. Botibol will certainly lose, and he is frantic.

Then a desperate but brilliant scheme comes to him: jump overboard! Someone will report it to the captain, the ship will stop, a lifeboat will be lowered, Botibol will be rescued, a precious unexpected hour or two will be added to the ship's delay, and Botibol will surely win the pool! But he certainly doesn't want to die.

The important detail is that a witness to the event must be established so that the captain will save him. He finds a nicely dressed older woman standing alone on the lower deck. He talks to her briefly and pleasantly, says he's going to exercise. He vaults over the rail shouting, "Help! Help!"

> When the first shout for help sounded, the woman who was leaning on the rail started up and gave a little jump of surprise. She looked around quickly and saw sailing past her through the air this small man dressed in white shorts and tennis shoes, spread-eagled and shouting as he went. For a moment she looked as though she weren't quite sure what she ought to do: throw a life belt, run away and give the alarm, or simply turn and yell. She drew back a pace from the rail and swung half around facing up to the bridge, and for this brief moment she remained motionless, tense, undecided. Then almost at once

she seemed to relax, and she leaned forward far over the rail, staring at the water where it was turbulent in the ship's wake. Soon a tiny round black head appeared in the foam, an arm was raised about it, once, twice, vigorously waving, and a small far-away voice was heard calling something that was difficult to understand. The woman leaned still farther over the rail, trying to keep the little bobbing black speck in sight, but soon, so very soon, it was such a long way away that she couldn't even be sure it was there at all.

After a while another woman came out on deck. This one was bony and angular, and she wore horn-rimmed spectacles. She spotted the first woman and walked over to her, treading the deck in the deliberate, military fashion of all spinsters.

"So *there* you are," she said.

The woman with the fat ankles turned and looked at her, but said nothing.

"I've been searching for you," the bony one continued. "Searching all over."

"It's very odd," the woman with the fat ankles said. "A man dived overboard just now, with his clothes on."

"Nonsense!"

"Oh yes. He said he wanted to get some exercise and he dived in and didn't even bother to take his clothes off."

"You better come down now," the bony woman said. Her mouth had suddenly become firm, her whole face sharp and alert, and she spoke less kindly than before. "And don't you ever go wandering about on deck alone like this again. You know quite well you're meant to wait for me."

"Yes, Maggie," the woman with the fat ankles answered, and again she smiled, a tender, trusting smile, and she took the hand of the other one and allowed herself to be led away across the deck.

"Such a nice man," she said. "He waved to me."

৪০ ❖ ৎৎ

SOME SHORT STORIES WOULD NEVER BE REMEMBERED EXCEPT FOR their last scene, like Anatole France's famous story "The Procurator of

Judea." In his latter years Pontius Pilate is being idly questioned about certain events that had occurred during his reign:

> But the man who had suffered exile under Tiberius was no longer listening to the venerable magistrate. Having tossed off his cup of Falernian, he was smiling at some image visible to his eye alone.
>
> After a moment's silence he resumed in a very deep voice, which rose in pitch by little and little—
>
> "With what languorous grace they dance, those Syrian women! I knew a Jewess at Jerusalem who used to dance in a poky little room, on a threadbare carpet, by the light of one smoky little lamp, waving her arms as she clanged her cymbals. Her loins arched, her head thrown back, and, as it were, dragged down by the weight of her heavy red hair, her eyes swimming with voluptuousness, eager, languishing, compliant, she would have made Cleopatra herself grow pale with envy. I was in love with her barbaric dances, her voice—a little raucous and yet so sweet—her atmosphere of incense, the semi-somnolescent state in which she seemed to live. I followed her everywhere. I mixed with the vile rabble of soldiers, conjurers, and extortioners with which she was surrounded. One day, however, she disappeared, and I saw her no more. Long did I seek her in disreputable alleys and taverns. It was more difficult to learn to do without her than to lose the taste for Greek wine. Some months after I lost sight of her, I learned by chance that she had attached herself to a small company of men and women who were followers of a young Galilean miracle worker. His name was Jesus; he came from Nazareth, and he was crucified for some crime, I don't quite know what. Pontius, do you remember anything about the man?"
>
> Pontius Pilate contracted his brows, and his hand rose to his forehead in the attitude of one who probes the deeps of memory. Then after a silence of some seconds—
>
> "Jesus?" he murmured, "Jesus—of Nazareth? I cannot call him to mind."

℀ ❖ ℁

THE PROVOCATIVE OPENING SCENE IS GOOD—

"It was now lunch time and they were all sitting under the double green fly of the dining tent pretending nothing had happened."

The chilling closing scene is even better.

Ernest Hemingway conceived most of his works in scene following scene; there are several memorable scenes in his short story masterpiece, "The Short Happy Life of Francis Macomber," but the final one is unforgettable.

Mr. and Mrs. Macomber, married for eleven quarrelsome years, are several days into an African safari. Francis has proved himself a total coward and has earned the further contempt of his beautiful but discontented wife, Margo, who loves him only for his money. She has already slept with the handsome white hunter, Wilson, and Francis knows it. On the last day, Macomber finds his courage and performs very bravely with a cape buffalo. Margo is upset because she feels he has shed his indecision, found himself, and she fears he will now divorce her.

In the final scene she is waiting in the car while the two men approach a clump of bushes where a wounded buffalo has taken refuge. Suddenly the animal charges. Macomber, firing, stands his ground even when the buffalo is almost upon him. Margo fires her rifle, presumably at the animal, but the bullet hits her husband at the base of his skull.

> Francis Macomber lay now, face down, not two yards from where the buffalo lay on his side and his wife knelt over him with Wilson beside her.
>
> "I wouldn't turn him over," Wilson said.
>
> The woman was crying hysterically.
>
> "I'd get back in the car," Wilson said. "Where's the rifle?"
>
> She shook her head, her face contorted. The gun-bearer picked up the rifle.
>
> "Leave it as it is," said Wilson. Then, "Go get Abdulla so that he may witness the manner of the accident."
>
> He knelt down, took a handkerchief from his pocket, and spread it over Francis Macomber's crew-cropped head where it lay. The blood sank into the dry, loose earth.
>
> Wilson stood up and saw the buffalo on his side, his legs out, his thinly-haired belly crawling with ticks. "Hell of a good bull," his brain registered automatically. "A good fifty

inches, or better. Better." He called to the driver and told him to spread a blanket over the body and stay by it. Then he walked over to the motor car where the woman sat crying in the corner.

"That was a pretty thing to do," he said in a toneless voice. "He *would* have left you too."

"Stop it," she said.

"Of course it's an accident," he said. "I know that."

"Stop it," she said.

"Don't worry," he said. "There will be a certain amount of unpleasantness but I will have some photographs taken that will be very useful at the inquest. There's the testimony of the gun-bearers and the driver too. You're perfectly all right."

"Stop it," she said.

"There's a hell of a lot to be done," he said. "And I'll have to send a truck off to the lake to wireless for a plane to take the three of us into Nairobi. Why didn't you poison him? That's what they do in England."

"Stop it. Stop it. Stop it," the woman cried.

Wilson looked at her with his flat blue eyes.

"I'm through now," he said. "I was a little angry. I'd begun to like your husband."

"Oh, please stop it," she said. "Please, please stop it."

"That's better," Wilson said. "Please is much better. Now I'll stop."

What a nice line that is: "I wouldn't turn him over."

A lesser writer might have reveled in a description of the bullet's gory havoc—and the image and effect on the reader would have been less than he conjures up for himself.

⚜

DASHIELL HAMMETT'S BOOK, *THE MALTESE FALCON*, APPEARED IN 1929 and the detective novel genre was changed forever. Though imitated relentlessly over the decades, it remains fresh, original with tough dialogue that still sparkles.

The one scene that everyone remembers is the unveiling of the black statuette of the falcon reputed to be made inside of solid gold and incredible ancient jewels.

Here is the way Hammett wrote the scene:

> Spade shut the door and carried the parcel into the living-room. Gutman's face was red and his cheeks quivered. Cairo and Brigid O'Shaughnessy came to the table as Spade put the parcel there. They were excited. The boy rose, pale and tense, but he remained by the sofa, staring under curling lashes at the others.
>
> Spade stepped back from the table saying: "There you are."
>
> Gutman's fat fingers made short work of cord and paper and excelsior, and he had the black bird in his hands. "Ah," he said huskily, "now, after seventeen years!" His eyes were moist.
>
> Cairo licked his red lips and worked his hands together. The girl's lower lip was between her teeth. She and Cairo, like Gutman, and like Spade and the boy, were breathing heavily. The air in the room was chilly and stale, and thick with tobacco smoke.
>
> Gutman set the bird down on the table again and fumbled at a pocket. "It's it," he said, "but we'll make sure." Sweat glistened on his round cheeks. His fingers twitched as he took out a gold pocket-knife and opened it.
>
> Cairo and the girl stood close to him, one on either side. Spade stood back a little where he could watch the boy as well as the group at the table.
>
> Gutman turned the bird upside-down and scraped an edge of its base with his knife. Black enamel came off in tiny curl, exposing blackened metal beneath. Gutman's knife-blade bit into the metal, turning back a thin curved shaving. The inside of the shaving, and the narrow plane its removal had left, had the soft gray sheen of lead.
>
> Gutman's breath hissed between his teeth. His face became turgid with hot blood. He twisted the bird around and hacked at its head. There too the edge of his knife bared lead. He let knife and bird bang down on the table where he wheeled to confront Spade. "It's a fake," he said hoarsely.
>
> Spade's face had become somber. His nod was slow, but

there was no slowness in his hand's going out to catch Brigid O'Shaughnessy's wrist. He pulled her to him and grasped her chin with his other hand, raising her face roughly. "All right," he growled into her face. "You've had *your* little joke. Now tell us about it."

She cried: "No, Sam, no! That is the one I got from Kemidov. I swear—!"

Joel Cairo thrust himself between Spade and Gutman and began to emit words in a shrill spluttering stream: "That's it! That's it! It was the Russian! I should have known! What a fool we thought him, and what fools he made of us!" Tears ran down the Levantine's cheeks and he danced up and down. "You bungled it!" he screamed at Gutman. "You and your stupid attempt to buy it from him! You fat fool! You let him know it was valuable and he found out how valuable and made a duplicate for us! No wonder we had so little trouble stealing it! No wonder he was so willing to send me off around the world looking for it! You imbecile! You bloated idiot!" He put his hands to his face and blubbered.

Gutman's jaw sagged. He blinked vacant eyes. Then he shook himself and was – by the time his bulbs had stopped jouncing – again a jovial fat man. "Come, sir," he said good-naturedly, "there's no need of going on like that. Everybody errs at times and you may be sure this is every bit as severe a blow to me as to anyone else. Yes, that is the Russian's hand, there's no doubt of it. Well, sir, what do you suggest? Shall we stand here and shed tears and call each other names? Or shall we"—he paused and his smile was a cherub's—"go to Constantinople?"

The line in the film borrowed from Shakespeare's *The Tempest*, that the statue was made of "such stuff as dreams are made on," doesn't appear in the book.

The novel goes on for some fifteen pages as Hammett ties up the loose ends. The final scene is between the beautiful but duplicitous murderess, Brigid O'Shaughnessy, and the detective, Sam Spade. She claims her love and her innocence, but Spade will have none of it.

"And you didn't know then that Gutman was here hunt-

> **Endings, endings! How to end the damn thing! What is the right ending? Writers seem to struggle more with endings than anything else.**

ing for you. You didn't suspect that or you wouldn't have shaken your gunman. You knew Gutman was here as soon as you heard Thursby had been shot. Then you knew you needed another protector, so you came back to me. Right?"

"Yes, but—oh, sweetheart!—it wasn't only that. I would have come back to you sooner or later. From the first instant I saw you I knew—"

Spade said tenderly: "You angel! Well, if you get a good break you'll be out of San Quentin in twenty years and you can come back to me then."

She took her cheek away from his, drawing her head far back to stare up without comprehension at him.

He was pale. He said tenderly: "I hope to Christ they don't hang you, precious, by that sweet neck." He slid his hands up to caress her throat.

In an instant she was out of his arms, back against the table, crouching, both hands spread over her throat. Her face was wild-eyed, haggard. Her dry mouth opened and closed. She said in a small parched voice: "You're not—" She could get no other words out.

Spade's face was yellow-white now. His mouth smiled and there were smile-wrinkles around his glittering eyes. His voice was soft, gentle. He said: "I'm going to send you over. The chances are you'll get off with life. That means you'll be out again in twenty years. You're an angel. I'll wait for you." He cleared his throat. "If they hang you, I'll always remember you."

How wonderfully Hammett has forever created the prototype of the tough private eye—two "tenderlys," plus a "soft, gentle" voice, plus "smile-crinkles" and a mouth-that-smiled, all colliding with devastating dialogue to his "angel."

Few films have ever followed a novel so faithfully as John Huston's 1941 masterpiece (the third movie made from the book). The entire cast is superb, but perhaps the standout was Sydney Greenstreet in his first film playing the "florid, sybaritic monster," Gutman. As the great film critic David Thomson has written: "It was a happy chance that his first film put him in the company of Peter Lorre, for they were inspired, tormenting company held together by some unspoken perversity."

They went on to appear in half a dozen more films together.

శు ❖ ల

IN GRAHAM GREENE'S 1949 THRILLER, *THE THIRD MAN*, DIRECTED by Carol Reed, Orson Welles plays the brilliant but crooked black marketer, Harry Lime. When writer Joseph Cotten confronts him on a Viennese ferris wheel, he delivers these ironic lines from a scene everyone remembers before Lime heads for the sewers in a futile effort to avoid the police. As you read them you must recall Welles' sarcastic and scathing delivery:

> You know what the fellow said: In Italy for thirty years under the Borgias they had warfare, terror, murder and bloodshed, but they produced Michelangelo, Leonardo da Vinci and the Renaissance. In Switzerland, they had brotherly love—they had 500 years of democracy and peace, and what did that produce? The—(pause)—cuckoo clock.

The amount of contempt with which Welles imbued the words *cuckoo clock* helped make the scene so memorable.

It has often been said that Welles himself wrote the scene, not Greene. The lines do not appear in Greene's novel, *The Third Man*.

Endings, endings! How to end the damn thing! What is the *right* ending? Writers seem to struggle more with endings than anything else, and there are few words of advice to be found anywhere.

Pusillanimous Hollywood often has "sneak" previews of wobbly films to find out which of the two filmed endings the viewers preferred, the one where the heroine tells the cad to get lost or the one where they get married; or whether the hero should die heroically or avoid the villain's compromise, and live happily ever after.

The worst esthetic crime of that sort ever committed, in my mind, was the emasculation of a great thriller, Daphne du Maurier's classic *Rebecca*. In the filmed version the protagonist doesn't murder his wife;

someone else does "because, you see, we can't have a popular star like Laurence Olivier be seen as a killer."

The most recent remake of a classic, *Pride and Prejudice*, has two different endings: in the English version, all is apparently chaste between the two lovers; in the American version Elizabeth and Darcy are in obvious coital bliss, including un-Austen-like kissing.

I was recently offered a substantial amount of money for an old property of mine for a film. The only catch was it had to have a happy ending. I turned it down, not easily, but *firmly*; it just wasn't right.

The ending should be satisfactory to the reader, based on what has gone before.

My hero had to die—it was the *right* ending, period.

14

L 'Envoi

So here are the 101 scenes. What can a beginning writer, young writer, aspiring writer, unpublished writer, glean from them?

Different ones will supply answers to different readers. At the best some clues, at worst some enjoyment.

But let me add what I have learned about how to write a successful piece of fiction. Ray Bradbury once gave a roomful of students at the Santa Barbara Writers' Conference perhaps the best one sentence piece of advice for a writer I've ever heard:

**"Find out what your protagonist wants
—really wants—desperately wants—
and when he or she gets up in the
morning just follow him or her."**

Your character must want something in order to come alive on the page. What is it? Revenge? Love? Help for a loved one? To win an important game? A coveted new job?

Whatever it is, it should be very important to the protagonist or it won't be to the reader. We must want the protagonist to attain his goal—we must want the antagonist to fail. And—so important—

**We must know, early on in the
story, who we are rooting for.**

If we are not rooting for anyone or anything, then we do not have a story.

Let us end the book, not with a great scene, but rather with some rules for writing by a great author.

Mark Twain wrote a scathing essay about James Fenimore Cooper, a popular writer in his day, showing how Cooper managed to break every one of these basic rules.

1. A tale shall accomplish something and arrive somewhere.

2. The episodes of a tale shall be necessary parts of the tale, and shall help to develop it.

3. The personages in a tale shall be alive, except in the case of corpses, and that always the reader shall be able to tell the corpses from the others.

4. The personages in a tale, both dead and alive, shall exhibit a sufficient excuse for being there.

5. When the personages of a tale deal in conversation, the talk shall sound like human talk, and be talk such as human beings would be likely to talk in the given circumstances, and have a discoverable meaning, also a discoverable purpose, and a show of relevancy, and remain in the neighborhood of the subject in hand, and be interesting to the reader, and help out the tale, and stop when the people cannot think of anything more to say.

6. When the author describes the character of a personage in his tale, the conduct and conversation of that personage shall justify said description.

7. When a personage talks like an illustrated, gilt-edged, tree-calf, hand-tooled, seven-dollar Friendship's Offering in the beginning of a paragraph, he shall not talk like a Negro minstrel in the end of it.

8. Crass stupidities shall not be played upon the reader by either the author or the people in the tale

9. The personages of a tale shall confine themselves to possibilities and let miracles alone; or, if they venture a miracle, the author must so plausibly set it forth as to make it look possible and reasonable.

10. The author shall make the reader feel a deep interest in the personages of his tale and in their fate; and that he shall make the reader love the good people in the tale and hate the bad ones.

11. The characters in a tale should be so clearly defined that the reader can tell beforehand what each will do in a given emergency.

A tale can be interesting, the characters believable—but the reader won't read enough of it to find this out if the language of the story is awkward or unclear. To prevent this, Twain's rules require that the author shall:

12. *Say* what he is proposing to say, not merely come near it.

13. Use the right word, not its second cousin.

14. Eschew surplusage.

15. Not omit necessary details.

16. Avoid slovenliness of form.

17. Use good grammar.

18. Employ a simple, straightforward style.

Amen, and may we all always abide by these rules!

One last anecdote:
Sinclair Lewis once was asked to address a large creative writ-

ing group at Columbia University. He strode out on the stage and immediately asked:

"How many of you out there are serious about being writers?"

They all raised their hands.

"Then," bellowed Lewis, "Why the hell aren't you home writing?"—and he walked off the stage.

So I say to you...

Why are you reading a book—why aren't you busy writing one?!

છ ❖ ભ

I *know* I have left out some of your favorite scenes; for that matter, I might well have left out some of my own, visions of which will come to me in the middle of the night all too soon.

If you have some favorites you feel strongly about, send them to me in care of the publisher:

Quill Driver Books
1254 Commerce Avenue
Sanger, California 93657

છ ❖ ભ

Index

Barnaby Conrad

An O. Henry Prize short story winner, he has written thirty books, including the bestsellers *Matador*, *Dangerfield* and *La Fiesta Brava*. Born in San Francisco, he served as American Vice Consul in Spain during World War II. As an amateur bullfighter he performed in Spain, Mexico and Peru over some fifteen years until badly gored in El Escorial, Spain. As a young man he worked as secretary to the novelist Sinclair Lewis in Williamstown, Massachusetts. He wrote a "Playhouse 90" script for John Frankenheimer, the screenplay for Steinbeck's *Flight*, and a Broadway play from his novel *Dangerfield*. He is the founder of the prestigious Santa Barbara Writers Conference, now in its thirty-fourth year.

Of his latest novel, *Last Boat to Cadiz*, William F. Buckley has written: "A master storyteller has done it again with a great tale."